Nikki Gemmell is the bestselling author of thirteen novels and four works of non-fiction, including *The Ripping Tree, Shiver, After* and *On Quiet*. Her books have been translated into twenty-two languages. She was born in Wollongong, New South Wales, and lived in London for many years, but has now returned to Australia. Her distinctive writing has gained her critical acclaim in France, where she's been described as a 'female Jack Kerouac'. The French literary magazine *Lire* included her in a list of the fifty most important writers in the world – those it believes will have a significant influence on the literature of the twenty-first century. Gemmell also pens a weekly column for the *Weekend Australian Magazine*.

NIKKI GEMMELL

Dissolve

hachette
AUSTRALIA

Published in Australia and New Zealand in 2021
by Hachette Australia
(an imprint of Hachette Australia Pty Limited)
Level 17, 207 Kent Street, Sydney NSW 2000
www.hachette.com.au

 A catalogue record for this
book is available from the
National Library of Australia

ISBN: 978 0 7336 4604 1 (hardback)

Cover design by Christabella Designs
Cover image courtesy of Arelix/Shutterstock
Author photograph by Kathy Luu
Text design by Bookhouse
Typeset in 12.2/17 pt Garamond MT Pro by Bookhouse
Printed and bound in Australia by McPherson's Printing Group

The paper this book is printed on is certified against the
Forest Stewardship Council® Standards. McPherson's Printing
Group holds FSC® chain of custody certification SA-COC-005379.
FSC® promotes environmentally responsible, socially beneficial
and economically viable management of the world's forests.

To all the women who've taught me
how to live over the years.

Thank you for lifting and supporting me.
I feel the strength in your arms.

1

The men in your life have never known how forensically you watch them. How you observe, scrutinise, marvel. Coldly. They are always prey. You have been doing this since you were fourteen or fifteen, when you began to know them in a different way; when they started to circle. They didn't realise how keenly they were watched. All the males who had so much power over your future.

You could not tell them that what they were imposing upon you felt inauthentic. Cruel. All the rules they were expecting you to adhere to, all they wanted you to be. To a teenage girl trying to navigate her way through a brave new existence it felt like fraud, of a monstrous, unfathomable kind. Because it seemed that they wanted you to be someone else. Your father, brothers, male teachers, early boyfriends, uncles: they all seemed to be expecting something different, and were trying, subtly, to change you. Shape you.

As you grew up you knew instinctively that you had to hide who you really were, as a survival tactic. Because the thumb of expectation pressed down upon you during those teenage years and into your twenties. And you wondered what lay beyond, when the great weight of that thumb was released, if ever it would be. You could scarcely imagine.

~

It doesn't matter who he is, this one you have in your sights now. There's no need to know his name, just that he is a writer. That's all. Let's call him W, for convenience sake. You're in your mid-twenties and want to be a writer yourself. But you do not consider yourself one, do not have the confidence to claim this mighty word for yourself. He is one loudly, smoothly, indubitably.

During this time Paul Keating is prime minister and Bill Hayden governor-general. In Spain, Christopher Skase is fighting against extradition in a Majorcan court and a fossil tree – the extraordinary Wollemi Pine – is found by a bushwalker, hidden in a pocket of bushland west of Sydney. The films *Muriel's Wedding* and *The Adventures of Priscilla, Queen of the Desert* are released amid much joy and national chuff. And among the crop of new Australian novels are Tim Winton's *The Riders*, Richard Flanagan's *Death of a River Guide,* Peter Carey's *The Unusual Life of Tristan Smith* and John Birmingham's *He Died With a Felafel in His Hand.* Muscular books all, sucking up the oxygen of fiction's new release schedule and spoken of as instant classics. It seems no one thinks to ask: where are the women?

W inhabits this world comfortably. It is a wonder to you. Perhaps this is one reason why you fall for him, quickly and completely, so soon after you meet.

~

'I can't do it.'

W is speaking softly, as if through thick, bubbled glass, in an innocuous Indian restaurant in Sydney's Kings Cross. Just four humble little words from the man you are about to marry. The chapel is booked. The bridesmaids organised. The first fittings have been carried out on an (audaciously iron grey) wedding dress. And W is the man you have invested all of your future in.

You have given up the town you've loved living in, for him; you've stopped trying to grab hold of a writing life, for him. And with these four hesitantly spoken words you feel your future disintegrating. Everything you had planned. All your certainties. Confidence. Resolve. You feel your entire self dissolving in this moment, the person you had so carefully created until this point.

'I can't go through with it. The wedding.'

You feel yourself becoming someone else, as you listen. Because in that moment all the foundations of a successful, shared existence of creativity have crumbled beneath you and you're not sure what will hold you up now, if anything. You've never known a failure like this.

Humiliation. Mortification. Never known the violence of such a blindsiding. And stretching before you now is an endless, stubbly world of aloneness and unloveability. Accompanied by a sense of having no idea what has just happened and a self-hatred at not being able to see. Anything.

Your cheeks burn with flame amid this very public rejection; your eyes sting. You will not be able to walk past this Indian restaurant for years afterwards. Yet in this moment you also feel a glimmer of the person you are meant to be. A girl, a woman, angry and flinty and determined and knowing. It is the person you really want to be but are never allowed to. Because there feels like such a violent disconnect between who you present to the world, and who you really are.

But first you have to back yourself away from the abyss opening up beneath you, a deep well of despair and self-revulsion that you want to be swallowed up by, and never emerge from. And you're not sure, in the reeling days afterwards, that you'll ever get to become that female you really want to be. Not sure if you'll ever have the courage for it. Because self-doubt is the cloak you've wrapped yourself in your entire life until this point.

～

Life can change in the sliver of a moment at a nondescript neighbourhood restaurant. It's what you do in the swirl of afterwards that defines you, how you carry yourself. It's what you do in the days that follow that can shape the rest of your life.

The abyss is beckoning. How can you face the world now? Your family, so joyful at your good fortune after so many years of restless singledom; your friends all seemingly firming into their settled lives; your colleagues who'd farewelled you so joyously, so recently, from the town you've loved more than any other in your life.

'I can't go through with it.'

He can't do the life so carefully planned together, the kids you'd both dreamed of, the house of books and coffee and laughter and clamour; your very own giggle palace. He stumbles through his explanations as if it's a reflection on who you are, the person you've so carefully been until this point. And now you're found wanting; the ideal of womanhood you thought you were meant to be. W tells you the wedding is happening too fast, despite eight months of preparation, he says it's too rushed and the 'money thing' between you is too uncertain. You're the regular wage-earner, with a job as a reporter for the Australian Broadcasting Corporation, he is a freelance writer. He says to wait a year and then see. Still go out, but just see if this can work. If it's what you both want, really. Then he waits for an answer.

You do not give it on that nondescript Tuesday night. You see before you, in the reeling silence, snatches of many things. The patterns repeated of your single mother and twice-married grandmother. The young woman fundamentally unloveable, too focused on her job and wage and the image of perfection she's created and cannot shake. The woman who's not attractive enough. Too interior, closed, odd and, above all, that ugly word: driven.

~

Many people around this crumbling young woman assume she has a healthy, almost obnoxious sense of self-belief, and it often feels like the world wants to bring her down a peg or two because of it. If only they knew. The insecurity, self-doubt, unease, the constant questioning. All you see right now is a girl too removed from normality; a girl who'll never be able to have and hold a man. All your self-loathing feels justified and has just been confirmed by the actions of this man; this older writer who's backing away, fast, from your future. And after all, if he doesn't love you enough – then why should you, or anyone else? You feel, overwhelmingly in this moment, wrong. But you've always felt somehow wrong. The world has repeatedly told you this.

Yet on this ragged night you also catch a glimpse of the woman you've never been. A woman contemplating the cage door and stepping out tentatively into an obscurity that's the beginning of an entirely new person. The one you've always wanted to be, perhaps, if you were ever brave enough. And if you were ever given enough anonymity to experiment. To loosen. But you've spent your entire life being conditioned to be a successful young lady, of the type men around you approve of. A young lady who's obedient and meek and calm, good and refined and quiet. Why be anything but that?

Yet, yet, why be that?

2

The desire to write feels like such a hesitant flame within you back then; insistent yet tremulous. Could you? The want so daring and audacious, yet monstrous too. Writing hurts. You've already gleaned this. It hurts the people around you as well as yourself. It flays you in public, strips bare your vulnerabilities, mortifies family and friends. And you're a pleaser. Is it all worth it? Could it ever be?

The writer Elizabeth Smart said a pen is a furious weapon that needs a rage of will. You're not sure you have the nerve for it. You have grit and determination but do not have the elixir of self-belief. Why would you? Your world doesn't encourage it. You wonder if you could ever make it as a writer, callously and meticulously existing on the coalface of living to record all that happens around you. You wonder who that kind of woman could be. Someone with a muscular and monstrous selfishness, surely, and women aren't allowed to be that. Surely.

Yet the urge feels like a glittering and beautiful darkness within that only you can see. It feels clean, like honesty. Yet veracity seems like such a transgression because the chilly, watching, assessing core of you is so submerged. Iceberged. Women aren't meant to say brutally honest things, aren't conditioned to be boldly truthful. The message being: what man would want us if we were?

You feel bound by what you are meant to be.

~

It is so easy to be snuffed by a failure to believe in yourself. That you can actually do this. Write. You are ready to believe anyone who says that you are no good at this creative malarky. Could you learn to trust your instinct? Perhaps it is what every woman must learn to do. Disentangle. Question. Push back. Surface into the light. Be who she really wants to be.

Why is it so hard for so many women to embrace the audacity of self-belief? It so often becomes just two slightly grubby, reducing little words for us. Because traditionally women are not meant to have a blazing sense of self-belief – of the kind that men are allowed. Traditionally we're not meant to boldly stride forth with daring and thrust and guile. Yet self-belief is an armour. It empowers us. To break through, achieve, get.

Growing up in deep suburbia in Wollongong, a steel and coal town south of Sydney, you saw that self-belief in a young girl was something akin to a grubby old coat to be shucked off and forgotten about in a cupboard – it had a certain odour to it. It was so forward, unfeminine, odd, wrong. As Henry James wrote of his Isabel Archer, in *The Portrait of a Lady*, 'she was liable to the sin of self-esteem'.

You were the daughter of a coalminer, as was your mother; your father and two grandfathers were all coalminers. You were meant to be quiet and mild and to conform to an unthreatening norm, to not stand out. And throughout your formative years the notion of grasping an audacious dream – and an intellectual one at that, like writing – was presented at various times as up yourself, deluded and a deeply unpleasant character trait for a girl. Yet you persisted. Quietly. Told no one of the urge coiled deep within.

It led to imposter syndrome, so prevalent in women back then and of course still. The term emerged in the seventies in a paper by US psychologists Pauline Rose Clance and Suzanne Ament Imes, who found that, despite outstanding academic and professional accomplishments, women who experienced the devilish, defeating impostor phenomenon often believed they weren't really bright – and had just fooled everyone who may have thought otherwise.

As women, we're meant to survive on less. Less success, money, autonomy, self-belief. Because self-belief leads a person to push ahead through life; to push away from circumstances that might not, actually, be the best for them. If you don't have self-belief you may well quieten, flatten and vanish, which to some people, of course, is helpful. Especially if they're used to having the power, all the time.

~

The composer Gustav Mahler's wife, Alma, was also a talented composer in her own right yet her husband stopped her creating music as a condition of marriage. He wanted only one composer in the family. 'There's such a struggle going on in me!' Alma wrote in her diary. 'And a miserable longing for someone who thinks OF ME . . . I've sunk to the level of a housekeeper!' Her husband's selfish stifling of her talent drove her to depression. He had won.

How are women meant to maintain a strong sense of self-belief in their talents, passions, drives, if the men around them fail to acknowledge these impulses; refuse to give women the space to expand, creatively? What does it do to the female psyche, to be so . . . muted?

~

For women, a lack of self-belief means we get good at surviving on less. It's an exercise in self-erasure. We have to learn to find our own unseemly self-belief, and embrace it. Yet how – when generations of women have been conditioned to believe it's somehow wrong, a fault – how can we not only find it but have an excess of it?

But back then, in your mid-twenties, in the year of the big boys publishing their muscular books you feel that your life will be somehow disfigured if you don't, one day, give the writing dream a go; if you don't heed that tiny flame of self-belief deep within you. That one day you can do this too. Write. Self-belief is the only thing that keeps you going, creatively. You have to ignore, again and again, all the voices around you telling you to stop. So many voices, usually male. And you could so easily obey all the sneerers, all the doubters and dismissers who want the self-belief disappeared from you; could so easily heed them and slip away into a quiet life rather than nurture that tiny glow of a something deep inside you. You could so easily give up.

~

A woman's self-belief is often challenged. It leads us to stop asking for pay rises. To agonise when we don't fill all the criteria for a promotion so we don't give it a shot – unlike lesser qualified men, who often just go for it. It leads to imposter syndrome.

We're not meant to leak a robust, masculine sense of self-belief. It should be kept secret. Not displayed under any circumstances, because females come to understand that it puts people off. But if we as women don't have it, if we are good and humble and obedient, how are we meant to get ahead in a world not built for our success?

3

Your desire is patient and particular. You do not know when it will strike, and it does extremely rarely. But it will lead you down paths you don't want to go or that aren't necessarily good for you. You learn that desire consumes focus and grit and strength, it lures you from a sure path. And it feels, in your mid-twenties, that biology will always fell you. There's a devouring urge to settle, in stillness, with a child at some point – even when you know it means the destruction of the blazing writing dream you've freighted so fiercely since girlhood. And in that moment of disintegration in the Indian restaurant you are caged, quite willingly; yoked to the wants of a man. A way of existing as a woman that is fierce and free isn't known to you yet. As a mother, writer, wife. You don't know how to grasp any of it, and don't have the courage for it.

The world back then didn't want a girl muscling in through the gates of power. It wanted to stop you being loud and driven and persistent and questioning; to just give up, to be silent and stop striving for something different. To not demonstrate intelligence in any way that was threatening to men.

If only they knew you always write it down. Everything. About them. The ones who dare get close.

~

In Year 8, at your all-girl convent school, your English teacher handed out journals. She tasked you all with writing every day in the freshly lined notebooks, without fail, anything at all. She would collect them every Friday, not to read but merely to check that they were being filled. She nurtured a habit that lasts you a lifetime. To this day your journals are crammed with little depth charges of observation; honesty bombs lined up, one after another, especially when it comes to men.

~

'You're always angry,' your mother told you once, in bewilderment, and that of course went into the journal too. Even women around you, who you admired, called you driven as if it was a dirty word. Odd, anti-female, slightly dangerous, something not to aspire to. Because that would make you different from the pack, would mark you out as singular and introduce the idea that their choices were somehow wanting, disturbing and constricting. An anathema to the soul.

You got the message, from your watchful teen years, that to be driven and focused and different as a girl was wrong. Unacceptable and unseemly. To not need the pack was appalling and strange. The fathers of school friends didn't like it, some friends didn't like it and felt threatened by it. Yet you were bewildered because this drive seemed to be expected of boys, of men. Focus and grit and hunger were applauded, as was ambition. It had been ingrained into them but for you, it was wrong. Why?

Virginia Woolf wrote to a friend in 1925, 'Men are all in the light always: with women you swim at once into the silent dusk.' The shock for you was that some women seemed to want this swimming into the dusk; for themselves and other women too. It was as if some females wanted all their sex bound and conforming and obedient; anything else was too challenging and terrifying. A woman unleashed. Imagine. The horror of it. All of the dusk-women's choices would be thrown into a harsh light by the blare of the strange and singular Other. The one who questions. Who is not meek or silent.

~

You were so invested in being liked back then, bound by the rules expected of young women. Another you existed alongside this story, for so many years, decades. A chafing, prickly, affronted and questioning you. Unlikeable perhaps, uncompromising.

17

W is at the heart of this story, as men so often are. Back then you were the sidekick. The experiment. Accessory. Muse. As women so often are. But finally you are writing this out, centring yourself in the narrative, and already you can feel an aversion to this. From yourself. What audacity, cheek. You're not important enough for this, says some censorious inner self. Women aren't meant to do this, be this. But, but. 'As I write,' Virginia Woolf declared in *A Writer's Diary*, 'there rises somewhere in my head that queer and very pleasant sense of something which I want to write; my own point of view . . .' Your own point of view.

Throughout your relationship with W you barely consider that. Your wants, your ambition, your need to be a writer, it all vanishes.

∼

It's as if love is the worst thing for you – for your self-worth and strength – because of how it will weaken you. Subsume, annihilate. This seems like a transgressive knowledge and you're not ready for it yet. Yet it feels like you have to pass through the fire and come out the other side, to understand.

∼

Before W breaks you, your life feels sorted. You are a single woman heading into your mid-twenties. You're living in Alice Springs and working as a radio reporter in the town's small ABC newsroom. On the day of arrival in that tough frontier place you swallow a fly and are told it's good for you by a fierce, desert-creased female anthropologist of singular abruptness. Your new neighbour.

It's a life of fresh wonder as you gulp the strange land and sky and desert smell, gulp all the new experiences around you. You move around town on an old bicycle with a journal always in your backpack alongside your reporter's notebook. There are trips out bush to visit mates who work for Indigenous art centres at Yuendumu and Ikuntji, eye-opening days in the Alice Springs courthouse and camping trips with your swag in dry riverbeds with a posse of new scientist friends. Your favourite place is to go where you've never been, so to be here is a dream. Curiosity is your fuel. There's so much difference to savour, and in your own country no less. The wings of wonder are spread wide. It's like you're living a perpetual weekend even though you're working hard on gruelling reporting shifts that begin at dawn. Yet you're beholden to no one here and in this gift of a strange land you unfurl.

You live in a stone share house with a red cement floor. It's owned by Robyn Davidson, the woman who walked four camels from the Centre to the sea and wrote a book about it called *Tracks*. She seems to have the perfect life: a desert bungalow in Alice with a writer's studio out the back, alongside a flat in London; it's a glamorously peripatetic existence that follows the summer sun across the earth.

You observe how this distant woman has carved a singular life for herself; how she's netted a spareness and expansiveness to live a fierce, lone writer's existence. It feels like she's living, as a woman, exactly how she wants to. She's done it triumphantly with a love for solitude, an unwillingness to compromise and an independent income. She's great mates with your anthropologist neighbour but she's not interested in her tenants, doesn't bother to get to know you, is polite but nothing more; there's a fierce wall of self-sufficiency fencing her off. Her life seems complete; it doesn't need the clutter of anything else. There's only one thing, of course, that could veer you from the dream of that life. Love.

4

You lost your virginity, at eighteen, to a would-be writer at university. You were both in first year at a fabled institution of sandstone arches and meet because of a shared love of theatre.

The gesture is what you remember the most on the night you lose your virginity. A gesture to his mates. He has taken you to a house, you don't know whose, where a group of his friends are relaxing in the lounge room. Four or five of them. The two of you peel off to a bedroom. It is quick. It hurts. Looking back, you're not wet, not aroused, it all happens too fast. You remember thinking, *Oh, that's it*, after all your years of yearning and wondering, desperate to shake off the burden of pesky, unwanted virginity. It had felt like a great encumbrance during your teenage years, an embarrassment; a burden almost every other teenage girl around you shared.

You had been mortified by your innocent state from fifteen onwards. You implied to any new girls you met that you were more mysterious than you ever were, that you had known boys at an outside-school drama camp or art class; you left it vague. This made you feel empowered, as if you'd stepped into a world they knew nothing of and were desperate to be part of; it made you feel you had something over them when you had nothing at all. At high school you buried yourself in class work and a close-knit group of six or so girls. It was a daggy, swotty posse dubbed the 'Birdbrains' by the popular, moneyed, predominantly blonde girls of your form. You were dark-haired and intense and extremely shy but learning to mask it; you were creating yourself.

The man – the boy-man – who takes your virginity has a voice that's confident, quick, declamatory. He doesn't seem to experience any social awkwardness, yet you feel tortured by it. Existing out in the world is hard, a shock after the cloistered teen years. It is hard to lift your eyes fully and boldly to others, hard to talk smoothly to men you're attracted to, hard to overcome the extreme, blush-inducing shyness. If this boy-man has any social anxiety about anything he never conveys it. He exists forcefully. At eighteen, nineteen. This is a marvel to you. You know no girls like this, no one so brazen. You think he's clever with words, dextrous, and he uses them as a sword to cut and jab and thrust and parry, silencing you with an eloquent and arrogant brilliance.

You know now it was tedium. He was entrancing no one but foolish young things like yourself; he was boring the rest. At the time you were dazzled by him. Convinced.

~

His gesture to his mates is the one sharp memory of that bleak night of virginity loss. It is made as the two of you leave the anonymous bedroom of the anonymous house. Your boyfriend walks out to his mates in the lounge room and raises his middle finger to them, obscenely, with a smirk of something like triumph. It's a blunt signalling, a private 'got her' moment. Between the lads. The shock of it, and your perspective pivots from that moment – he isn't doing this for you at all. He's doing it for them. For their approval.

Memories of that night: the sawing away at your unwet entrance and an utter absence of tenderness and of anything approaching an orgasm. Your growing intrigue, and revulsion. You feel grubbied and cheap, little more than worthless. This is just a moment of conquest to him, which has to be shared with the lads and you feel weirdly peripheral to the moment of capture; the sidelining feels intentional and immoral and utterly normal. Yet you've just given away one of the most precious things you have: a secret, deeply private and complex sexuality, alongside your nakedness which you've never given to anyone. And you are extremely modest. You've given it all away in the heat of a moment, for what? You aren't sure.

~

So. You have been initiated into adulthood at last yet you wonder why you don't feel better or older or more confident, you wonder why you feel reduced. And there was an utter absence of the thing you crave the most. Tenderness. Simone de Beauvoir said the first penetration is always a rape, and if not that then certainly a violation, in its coldness and its absence of tenderness, and you recognise this. Because on the night you lose your virginity you realise a startling truth: that you are just a hole, to them. You have been erased in all other aspects. At no time did the boy-man ask what you wanted, at no time did he consider your own sexual pleasure.

The relationship stutters on for a few months until he finds someone else and, with something like relief, you go your separate ways. You have to wait years before you feel cherished by a lover. You don't experience transcendent sex until deep into your twenties, several partners down the track.

~

The boy-man who takes your virginity is extremely confident that he will be a writer. This is intriguing, even back then. His confidence that a writing career will happen. There will be accolades and adulation, writers' festivals and write-ups, and in the thick of early togetherness there are plans for you to accompany him on his feted odyssey.

You're intrigued by the entitlement surrounding his dream, the perceived rightness of this journey for an articulate young man who blazes intelligence and good reading. It is his destiny. Everyone around him seems to recognise it. He is on a smooth, sure path. For him there will be no impediment, and no self-doubt. None that he shows you, at least.

~

Your own writing dream is a secret smoulder of a thing barely voiced in the headwind of his certainty. You are blighted by the curse of perfectionism, as so many high-achieving young women around you are, and a writing contract and all the subsequent traps and failures of publication is something you could never control. Why would you vocalise something that feels almost impossible and, at the least, extremely gruelling, with no promise of a reward at the end of it? You've never had anyone tell you it was meant to be; that you're destined to be a writer. The audacity of such a ridiculously ambitious and indulgent dream, from a coalminer's daughter from the suburbs, *how dare you.*

This boy-man who takes your virginity is your first experience of men drowning women out, erasing them, with their confidence.

5

Between eighteen and twenty-three you succumb, intrigued, to a series of one-night stands. Most often with fledgling actors and painters and filmmakers, drifters and dreamers in the creative life, yet it always strikes you as sex of bleak and unbearable loneliness; a jagged type of aloneness you've never felt before in your life, especially not when by yourself. You fall into desultory sex again and again to see if the pattern can be broken. But it never is.

You're not attracted to these men. You're attracted to the idea of a fresh experience – that this time it will work, surely – and by a curiosity that you may orgasm, finally. But no, and again no. You begin to wonder if you're defective in some way. Why is this all so hard? And the men you're deeply attracted to you can't talk normally to, you're clotted with awkwardness and shyness. The ones you can talk to you cannot imagine anywhere near your naked body and are revolted by the thought. As for the ones you do sleep with, you arrange yourself underneath them as if a camera on the ceiling is looking down upon you both; silently and secretly art directing a performative response.

Then afterwards you write the bleakness down.

~

'What are you thinking?' becomes the question asked most often by these men you sleep with. You do not tell them, can't, it would be too cruel. That you didn't come. That you hated it. That you're not attracted to them. That you're unsure about the politics of power and control in the bestowing of a blow job; why does it feel so close to humiliation? That you wanted it all to end sooner, faster. And that on these bleak nights of aloneness it is their sense of entitlement that intrigues the most; their expectation that you'll buckle to their desire for sex, eventually, and they will have you after all. In their world of unthinkingly male-centred sex.

You feel superior to them, watching and judging and waiting, before you move on to the next fuck then the next, with long stretches of alone in between. The coldness of the observing reminds you of the female protagonist in Marguerite Duras's *The Lover*, who realises that 'he doesn't understand her, that he never will, that he lacks the power to understand such perverseness. And that he can never move fast enough to catch her.' If only they knew how few of them you were attracted to. Whether you are or not doesn't seem to be factored into the equation, by any of them.

~

At sixteen you won a role in a film shot in far northern New South Wales, a long way from your Sydney home. The movie never sets the world on fire but the experience is instructive on many levels, about men most of all. At the time, your parents have no idea what goes on in the cloistered world of a film set. You win the role through a drama teacher at school and are sent off for weeks on location by yourself because neither of your parents can afford the time off work. The producers assure them you'll be well looked after; they provide a tutor to help with schoolwork. You're put up in the local pub along with various members of the cast and crew.

You are the quintessential swotty teenager drowning in teenage body insecurities, convinced you're too spotty and fat and too deeply unattractive for anyone of the opposite sex. You have no desire for that distracting world anyway. You're on this film set to act in the role of a thirteen-year-old in the 1940s and to keep up with your school studies remotely. You are focused, wide-eyed and earnest.

None of this stops some of the men involved in the film trying to get at you. Most act exemplarily, but there's an actor and crew member who treat you as something different. Prey. A challenge, a conquest, an intrigue, a right. Fresh meat. You watch them; you note.

You are, in that old-fashioned word, 'pestered' by these men, who are at least twice your age. One comes to your hotel room door, sometimes several times a night and always very late. He begs for a kiss, or to be held, with the expectation of something else no doubt. An actor who's married appears with just a towel around his waist and an obvious erection under it. You have never seen such a ludicrous thing and don't want to. You're here for work, you're getting paid, you have to do this job properly, you are not attracted to this man and you have to rise before dawn. Doesn't he get that?

And, from what you know, you have to be attracted to someone to do anything like what he wants. Don't you? Isn't that the way? The code? You certainly aren't attracted to any of these men, to almost no man in fact. You just want this actor to go away, all of this pestering to stop.

In the end – after a week or so of a ridiculous, nightly ritual of this man coming to your door and begging – he is sobbing. You recognise instinctively that the only way to be rid of him for good is to put him to sleep in his own bed and tuck in his blankets and soothe him like a mother would a child, because that's what he has begged you to do if you'll give him no sexual favours. You do it just the once – soothing, murmuring, petting – to be rid of him.

Men, and their insistent wants. You are learning.

～

A technician on the crew also comes to you repeatedly; again, you turn him away. He's in his late twenties and handsome in a conventional sense, but this means nothing to you; you're always attracted to the unconventional. The courage in difference. There's also the young apprentice who is gentle in his fumbling attempts but, once again, you don't want anything to do with him. You have nothing in common with these men, no mind in common – and that's the crucial factor for you. Do they not get that? Why do they think you'll be remotely interested in them? Perhaps they think it doesn't matter if you are or not. But why do they persist in the face of your constancy; does your will matter here at all?

As a sixteen-year-old – who has never done anything sexual in her life – you find these experiences disconcerting and flabbergasting and odd. Is this what men are? So vulnerable, babyish, needy. So . . . obvious. It fills you with sadness and horror that you're being seen as a mere receptacle for these males; a comfort blanket, a means to fill a sexual need. Nothing more. Only the young apprentice is interested in getting to know you further, to know your mind; the older men don't want to have actual conversations with you. That isn't the point. They expect a willingness or at least an acquiescence. Why are they so sure, so entitled? You are intrigued. Coldly. It is an experience.

You have spent your teenage years reading *Jane Eyre* and *Wuthering Heights* and *Little Women* and *My Brilliant Career* and *The Getting of Wisdom* – stories by women, about women. And about connections between couples. Yet this feels like another thing entirely.

You never tell anyone. You are embarrassed for these men, sorry for them, don't want to get them into trouble. Want somehow to protect them from their pitiable weakness and oddness. They feel like a minority but their modus operandi is disturbingly similar. Pester, harass, push themselves into your space without consideration of how uncomfortable it might make you feel – and wait for their reward. How have they been raised, to expect this of a schoolgirl? It is as if they believe it is their right. And you feel sure the people of the film set are aware of what's going on, and are collectively turning a blind eye to it. No woman checks in, asks you how you are.

What happens on that set fascinates and galvanises and changes you. Throughout your working life you are never 'pestered' again; you never allow men like that a sliver of an opening. Because you recognise them now – as predators. They saw you as prey, and you will never allow a man to think that of you again.

~

You never make it as an actress. A friend in the industry says to you soon after the film's release, 'There are faces for film, and then there's yours, and some just don't work for the camera.' His careless, mean-spirited words flatten you, they cast a seed of doubt within and you lose the fire in your acting belly. You believe him implicitly, because your own self-esteem is so fragile. But luckily you have another more urgent and more autonomous dream up your sleeve. To write.

Many men try and stop that one over the years, too. To silence your voice, diminish it, but you learn to trust your instincts, to endure.

You persist.

6

In 2016 that astounding blip on the historical landscape, Donald Trump, veered the conversation for women and in doing so did us all a service. Because long after the minutiae of the grubby, dispiriting 2016 US election campaign had been forgotten, we remembered how the conversation changed during his presidency. Trump's boast about his unasked-for gropings of any handy piece of female meat prompted women the world over to think afresh about the times, the many times, when they too had been reduced by male attention. When they had not spoken up because this is just what men did. Trump's casual cruelty towards women – and the way he seemed to get away with it – opened up a platform for many women to publicly share their own experiences.

Women began talking. Out of disgust, despair, recognition, fury. About Trump and the men like him who had always gotten away with it. About all those times they'd been touched when they hadn't wanted it, all those times they'd been told to smile or cheer up or that they lacked a sense of humour. 'It's just words, love.' 'Lighten up.' All those times they'd been drowned out in a way they didn't want. Good men alongside many women spoke in horror about the spectacular dinosaurosity of the Donald in all his red-blooded, pussy-grabbing tawdriness. First came the horror, then the anger. Because men like that were still getting away with it.

Women don't easily forget the times when they're the victim of unwanted male intrusion. A pushing into their space, serenity, equilibrium. It often starts young. When you were six a slightly grubby, overweight neighbourhood boy several years older coaxed you into the bushes and put his hand down your underpants and made you feel ashamed, aflame – yet you told no one. Why? It was your secret shame, *your* shame, not his. You grew up thinking this is what boys are. You told no one because no one did back then. Who would believe you anyway? Who would care enough?

You never spoke to anyone of the flatmate who rail-roaded you into a bleakly ugly one-night stand when you were twenty. Or the male friend who asked you to watch a TV programme with him, then ran his hand up your thigh while you sat next to him, frozen and stricken. Why would you? It was just men being men and your discomfort meant nothing in a time when the word consent had little currency. You grew up neither disliking these predators nor thinking they were wrong, nor detaching from them as companions. Why have we, as a society, enabled women to believe this; to expect this surrendering from them? Yet you can't wipe the memories. The shame, awkwardness, embarrassment; the times when you were made to feel somehow . . . less. Than them. Than your usual self.

But the world is changing. A girlfriend's daughter in Year 3 receives a 'dick pic' on Snapchat from a boy aged twelve. The mother is mortified, furious, and enabled. She feels empowered to say no, this is not on, you do not violate my daughter's innocence like this. The boy's parents are told, the incident dealt with. The boy is disciplined for his own future protection as much as anything else. He needs to know that his behaviour is now unacceptable. We are all learning. Women especially are becoming bolder in teaching the boys in their lives to be something different, something better. To be aware.

~

In your early twenties, a gay man asks you to marry him. A dear friend, your best friend. You say yes, impetuously, then mull it over and say no. For in the story of the man who leaves his long-wedded for another man, you always think of the woman. She's often left behind in the media narrative; the celebratory story of the courageous husband who's come out finally after decades of hetero-sexual marriage, when his leap into authenticity is rightly applauded. For him, it's about revelling in sexual freedom and release for quite possibly the first time in his adult existence. But what of the woman who has given so much of her emotional and sexual life to the man?

The ex-Liberal politician Michael Yabsley came out after decades of marriage to his wife, Susie. They have two children. Yabsley, in his mid-sixties, explained that he'd lived with denial for a very long time, perhaps like a lot of people in his age group. He said theirs was a happy marriage but not an authentic one, and that his sexuality had become the elephant in the room. He got to the point where he wanted to live the years he had left in the way he truly wanted to. The media story was dealt with sensitively, but while we heard from him in a beautifully compassionate way we didn't hear from Susie at all.

The 57-year-old British television presenter Phil Schofield came out around the same time, after twenty-seven years of a seemingly happy marriage. He explained he knew he was gay when he wed, but he realised that after decades of marriage he had to be completely honest with himself. In a brief statement, his loyal wife, Steph, said that as a couple they had faced the most emotionally painful time in their marriage; a statement that masks, you suspect, a wellspring of pain.

The organisation Women Partners of Bisexual Men helps women with partners who have come out, and has released a book on that situation – *There's Something I Have to Tell You*. It features interviews with twenty women. The theme that emerges: 'He stole my life.' In the wake of their husband's disclosure some women describe feeling like widows. One, Beth, talks of seventeen years being stolen from her; another, Lucy, speaks of an enormous physical impact – tremors, hair falling out and dramatic weight loss. 'I kept thinking: I'm dying,' she says. 'The only man who'd ever been attracted to me actually hadn't been, so all those horrible thoughts I'd felt about myself were actually true.' Elizabeth reflects on the women these men often marry. 'There's a stereotype that closeted men seek out a certain type of woman because we have qualities of acceptance, tolerance, understanding, empathy – but even if it's true, you don't want to feel like you're gullible.' Her anger is directed at the culture surrounding her husband, as well as his family, for not letting him be who he really wanted to be. 'It was like he didn't know how to be gay.'

Within the media story of married men coming out later in life, the woman's perspective is so often a nagging absence. Yet it's a narrative that may largely disappear as societal changes mean there are fewer closeted gay men among us; fewer women who find themselves left behind, or worse – realise that they were roped into marriage for conventionality's sake.

It's that sensibility which prevented you from marrying your gay best friend, from a deeply Catholic family, all those years ago. He made you feel like a shopfront. Marrying you would be a way of avoiding what he couldn't confront himself, and your own feelings seemed immaterial to his narrative. Where were your own wants and desires in the story; the vividness of your emerging sexuality? You were erased. Your wants unconsidered. You were not given the space to be who you really wanted to be. An authentic, honest, thinking, sexually empowered woman.

His proposal felt like a monstrous selfishness.

~

With the #MeToo movement there was a groundswell of anger from women – we do not want our daughters to go through what we have gone through. All the little jabbings and pricks throughout our lives, all the little brushed-off violations. Recently a man accosted a woman behind the counter of your local milkbar. His hairy belly was falling over skimpy shorts. 'It's Sunday,' he declared to everyone and no one waiting patiently in the crowded space. 'How about a free hug, love? Free hug Sunday.' His voice was loud and intrusive, as if everyone was meant to collude with his boorish sentiment; get a laugh out of it.

Yet not a single person smiled at the objectifying of this quietly appalled and dignified young woman by an obnoxious, obese, middle-aged man. He was making her feel uncomfortable as she stood patiently behind the counter, saying nothing, yet he didn't care. He was silenced by the rest. His behaviour wasn't 'just words'. It's never 'just words'. It's everyday assaults on a woman's serenity that make us flinch, that halt us in our tracks, annoy us and distract us. Women are conditioned to rarely show any of this but these men are on the wrong side of history now. The conversation is shifting; these men of the past are being left in the world's wake.

7

There are vast swathes of aloneness. Months, years of them, in your late teens, early twenties. Times when you catch sight of a couple in a park and your heart flinches with envy and longing and despair that you will never know this. There are New Year's Eves where you don't go out but paint furiously in your Kings Cross bedsit in Sydney instead; angry, expansive, colour-saturated canvases. There are Christmases of awkward questions from extended family, 'When are you going to get a boyfriend, love?' 'Are you happy?' And always there's the shrug, the smile and the need to escape.

At twenty-two you have a work romance with A, a colleague at the ABC, but you're better suited as mates than lovers. He loves Canberra and all the hurly-burly of federal politics; you love adventuring. The gulf between you feels too extreme. He will never move to a wild frontier place for you; you will never move to the likes of Canberra for him. You love him as a friend, your closest, and at twenty-three you part amicably. Into another desert, of sex.

~

Panic is swallowing you. That you're unloveable. Prickly and picky, too focused on career, too driven. You needed to cultivate looseness but don't know how. The other, wherever that is, becomes your flint, your spark. To compensate for your lack of a relationship you seek the life of the neophiliac, in love with fresh experience and constantly seeking the new. You move from Sydney to Darwin to Alice Springs. It's an odd career path for a journalist because traditionally the trajectory is from the smaller place to the city: the news nerve centre. But you're not interested in making reporting your life. You want something riskier, and freer. You have your fiction notebooks alongside your reporting ones.

'She ignored whatever did not interest her,' Annie Dillard wrote in *The Maytrees*. 'With those blows she opened her days like a piñata. A hundred freedoms fell on her.' That sentiment is your tuning fork into another life.

~

Then you meet him. You're to drive a freshly purchased car from Sydney to Alice Springs but need a driver who can help you get the hang of the manual gears, as you've only ever driven an automatic. The car is a white Holden ute you've purchased from your father for ten thousand dollars. You ask around for someone, anyone, who can teach you how to drive it and who wants a ride to Alice Springs, almost three thousand kilometres away. Someone who's patient, who won't infuriate you along the way.

'He's a great storyteller,' explains a mutual friend from Alice by way of introduction. 'He's tall and cool and kind of cute-looking.' W is her ex-boyfriend. You don't have a problem with this. Your friend says that W lives in a book-crammed garret in a cool inner-city suburb and is actually managing the impossible dream of making a living as a writer. You're intrigued.

He's a freelancer who writes across magazines and newspapers and composes poetry and has plans to write a novel some day. Already he seems to embody the Baudelairian myth of the artist, one of those heroes of modern living who live on a higher, headier plane than the rest of us. Your money situation, on the other hand, is steeped in boring practicality. A regular wage, superannuation, and a new mortgage on a two-bedroom flat in Kings Cross. You want to write novels, to finally give the dream a go, yet don't know how to support yourself while doing it. You're financially cautious, careful. You've been raised by a single mother who's always impressed upon you the need to make money for yourself, to never rely on a man when it comes to finances because then they have too much control over you. And that's what she fears the most – a controlling man. Your feminist mother wants you to not be distracted by males and their wants, because she believes they can make a woman weak and subservient and needy and compromised; and that's how, perhaps, they'd really like women to be.

You don't have the courage to leave your ABC job, to give the dream a go. Growing up in suburban Wollongong has made you hungry for a comfortable life. You have to be poor and envious – with a perspective from the outside looking in – to understand the compulsive need for comfort and the relentless hunger that can drive a disadvantaged person onward, and up, and out.

A public service job with the national broadcaster fills the brief for you, but after several years of gruelling shiftwork you're bone tired. It's depleting your inner life. Sapping your creativity. It feels like so much that you're witnessing as a journalist is possible fuel, one day, for fiction but you have no time to write creatively within the thick of the shiftwork. It feels like your soul is being swamped.

~

This potential driving instructor is a writer, an actual published one. The boy-man who took your virginity never quite launched himself into his projected career of literary festival panels and book prizes, even though it had seemed a sure bet at the time. His confidence had galloped ahead of him. But this fresh man feels like a step into the big league. You've never met a 'proper' writer before.

Every young, male, would-be writer you've met has had this strong vision of their uniqueness; it seems central to who they are. The Writer, destined for huge things, with the various people around them like stars orbiting in the firmament of their brilliance. You, on the other hand, are invisible in the face of all this. No one encourages you except for a handful of older, established writers who quietly accept your work in their literary magazines – like the poet Les Murray who publishes your first story at nineteen. You've had a dribble of acceptances from various Australian literary journals ever since, perhaps one a year, but it's enough to keep the tiny flame within you secretly burning. You don't tell anyone in your wider world. There's no one to tell, to boast to; no one who'd understand.

And you quietly suspect that if you declare your own raging writing ambition too strongly the world will chide you for it. Grind your dream underfoot, offer a corrective. You know instinctively to keep the bright blazing kernel of the dream tight within you. Your confidence is fragile, easily shattered, and it feels like this writing business is all about confidence. Your short story acceptances must have been flukes. Surely. Yet you persist. Quietly.

~

The lovers in your life who are creative have no idea how closely you observe them. This is not your story, it is his story. He directs it, controls it, he calls the shots of the narrative. But hidden inside you is a hard little tin foil ball of determination. The bullish male ego does not see this side of you at all. This determination to somehow be centred in your own narrative reminds you of the night you lost your virginity. The viciousness in the gesture of the raised middle finger to the lads. That was not your story either, it was his, the story of a man's interaction with his mates. How he made you peripheral to that experience seems almost impossible, yet he did. You were just a female body, a hole, a conquest. You weren't seen.

~

'What are you thinking?' No, all the past lovers didn't need your honesty. They wouldn't have liked it, and it would've made your path through the world they'd created for themselves all the more difficult. What were you thinking? That you felt smarter and stronger and more together and focused than the man in front of you trying to penetrate your mind, but you were never allowed to articulate that. And the world wouldn't let you show it. They could penetrate your body but not your mind, that was a survival instinct. Because you knew that to be loud and abrasive and honest could cost you jobs and relationships as a young woman. It could make you that dreaded word – unlikeable. Unemployable. Annoying. Yet the suppression of your voice and intrigue and rage didn't feel authentic. So you turned inward, to the interior, like a submarine sinking silently beneath the waves. To your journals and your secret writing, to voice your bewilderment.

Katherine Mansfield wrote a battle cry of female authenticity when she declared that she wanted to be all she was capable of becoming. You could never attain that with the fledgling writer you lost your virginity to. His want for the creative life was too loud, thrusting, dominating. You understood that your role was as sidekick, facilitator, muse. Distraction fuck. And it was accepted because all you wanted back then was love. Yet during those years of exploring the landscapes of creative relationships you suspected that love and a successful, focused artistic career could never coexist peacefully – for a woman. It seemed that the world was set up to keep questioning young women like you in their place.

If you want to be a good, acceptable woman – someone your convent high school would be proud to call their own – you grow to understand that you must make yourself smaller and quieter, you must soften your voice and anger and wants. Yet you chafe against the bit of belonging. *Get me out* is the constant, silent mantra when too much normality closes over you. The judgement of small worlds, the sneer at difference, the fear of the Other.

You learn the rules you must follow. Mainly, an adherence to the rules of that club called 'second best', otherwise known as the woman's lot. The expectations: you must not upstage a male nor question, you mustn't be flashy or loud or show off or dominate. You must never hurt a man's feelings or articulate painful truths. You must inhabit the periphery, never the centre. You must submit to being bound into the club of belonging and obedience.

~

You meet W, the writer, at a cool homewares store and café in inner Sydney. There's a business arrangement underpinning the impending trip. You need someone who has the patience to teach you a car's gearstick, and he wants to get to your town for a story. A hitchhiker with benefits, so to speak.

You bring along your gay friend who asked to marry you once. W is late. You're jumpy, waiting, don't do late; it rubs up too close to rudeness. Suddenly W is looming before you. 'Nikki?' he enquires hesitantly. 'Yeah,' you respond and slide into conversation, smoothly, talk is easy with this one. It's a bonus because conversational banter often doesn't flow, especially if you're attracted to someone; you're too shy and awkward and self-conscious for it. But with W there are wisecracks about journos and deadlines and his desire to write his first novel, all barely five minutes into the conversation. You relax into the easiness.

And yes, you're attracted. Because it feels that this very cool writer is everything you're not. You do not tell him you have a secret passion to write too. A passion that's been snuffed over the years as reporting deadlines and morning shifts and the carrot of promotions take over; that safe, sorted life that's settling like cement around you.

~

A girl arrives. She breezily joins your table. His girl — who knows? — he doesn't say. A nick of disappointment. She's tall and willowy and nonchalant in her slimline vintage jeans and t-shirt over a Birkinesque A-cup. It's the dreamed-of silhouette, everything you're not. You look at your watch, you have to go soon. You've seen enough, this will work. 'I see he's going to be in good hands.' W's friend smiles right at you, into you. He grins softly, chuffed. 'Yeah, it's going to work.' You smile, it is.

But his world, their world — with its seemingly effortless, inner-city, vintage store vibe — feels unattainable to you. You're a product of the suburbs of industrial Wollongong and now live in an outback town of twenty-five thousand people. The way these people carry themselves feels impossible. You'd be an imposter in their world, always pretending. With W it's the mirrored sunglasses, the haircut the right side of long, the vintage airline bag slung over his shoulder, the worn corduroy jacket.

Do you dare? It feels like your life has been poised until this moment, that you've been waiting for this kind of man your entire life. To teach you. He's a fair few years older; he's living your dream. 'There is no fool like a woman in need of a man,' Doris Lessing wrote in *Walking in the Shade*. 'A man, that is, to have and to hold.' And you are galloping into your mid-twenties and so ready for it.

Hillary Clinton once remarked that as soon as a man put his arms around her, as a young woman, she was gone. And you feel you could be too; feel so ready to embrace that annihilation. With the right man. You're consumingly desperate for it, ready to toss everything away for that one thing only: love. It feels like surrender and you'll happily do it.

8

A sunny Monday. October. The day of departure. Your mother's flat in Sydney.

Alice Springs is three days' drive away and you're flat on your back under your new ute, preparing with great chuff. Your father has deposited this car to your mother's apartment with a twinkle in his eye; he loves any excuse to be back in her world. You're securing the slipping numberplate with a screwdriver and scissors and string, feeling sexy-desert-strong as you tie and screw and lift boxes into the tray of the ute; a woman in control and proud of her bush vehicle with its high four-wheel drive tyres.

W saunters down the driveway, long and lean and out of place around your mother's dreary, suburban block of flats. 'Oh, here's W,' she remarks like she's always known him, and in a way she has. His type. She bustles you both upstairs, revelling in the young things, pulling out bits and pieces of food and offering them up. She's never as zealous with domesticity when it's just you. She flurries together a lunch pack of vegetable pie and chocolate biscuits, scurrying and fussing. Straight up, W tells you both he has a piece in a current fashion magazine. Your mother happens to have a subscription, it's your annual birthday gift; she dives onto the latest issue with glee and finds W's piece. You all pore over the splayed pages, exclaiming and praising. You can read your mother's thinking, *Ah yes, this is something to tell the friends, something good.* You hit the road three hours late with him driving. He stalls the car as your mother waves you off. 'Oh no, I wanted to impress her.' You laugh, get it. She's formidable beneath the easy charm and W senses it.

He drives you to his inner-Sydney share house. It's all uni-type clutter and dankness and a toilet smelling of urine and a flatmate having cereal at midday. You like the grungy buzz of the place, it's so removed from where you are now, deep in your world of grown-up shiftwork and responsibility. This reminds you of what you've lost. A free, creative, meandering kind of existence, a getting-up-at-midday life. You feel the lure of a different way.

'I like to be cosmopolitan,' Annie Ernaux wrote to a friend at nineteen. 'I would like to visit the whole earth and love it all.' And that is you during your teens and your twenties. There's so much living, experiencing, marvelling to be done and you wonder how you'll cram it all in. You want to seize every morsel of every novelty you can; new countries and cities, fresh landscapes and people. Until, possibly, this.

~

Beyond the city stop-start W and you slip headlong into conversation. It's like a thrill of cold water from a swimming pool you've dived into too soon in the season; it's good, fresh, hits. Relationships are established early on. He's just out of one that wasn't working, it never connected. You're pleased. His companion from the café is a sister-friend and nothing to worry about. As for your own relationships, there's nothing to report. Long stretches of alone, a long time since anything, the way is clear.

You both dive quickly into novels, art, film. There's none of the awkwardness of cracking on, this feels like a workmanlike arrangement that's cutting straight to fundamentals. Connecting and clean. As your ute climbs out of the city, up through the Blue Mountains, you feel plumed with lightness. Shedding burdens, shedding skins, diving into the new. Again.

~

You wonder about this fresh type of man, who's just told you he's never travelled overseas and has lived in only two places his entire life. You wonder because curiosity is your fuel. You want to gulp the world, open your mouth wide and tip it down your throat. Your favourite thing is to go where you've never been. And you've never done this iconic drive before, from city to desert, yet during it you're noticing W most of all. Turning inward, arrowed, to one particular man. For what feels like the first time in your life.

~

You don't talk to W of your bullish need to write; you mention you'd like to be a novelist one day but not how ferocious that desire is. It feels like a ruthless, glittery darkness coiled within you. A truth bomb waiting to explode. You dream of writing anonymously, with a steely honesty, so no one will ever be hurt. Because as a young woman you're a pleaser and that binds you to a servitude you don't actually want.

~

You push the ute on into the night, getting the hang of the manual gear shifts on long stretches of lone highway. You blink at the surreal disappearing road ahead that stretches on to Nevertire, a natural pit stop. Sudden headlights in front of you flash hard at your forgotten high beam. The car passes and you feel it contemplate, do a U-turn, and follow you on this long, empty highway. A shiver of a chill. A mutual decision to stop at Nevertire. A tremble, deep in your belly, as you think of sharing a room with this man at whatever pub you can find. There's no question of securing two rooms, you're both watching your money too much. The car following you drops away, is lost to the black, and you finally unclench.

~

Where is the sex in real life that's in your head, you wonder. That you conjure up night after night to tumble you into sleep. Where is the sex with you at the centre of it? It's never happened. In real life you're always on the periphery of a male-centred experience, not active, not demanding, instead arranging yourself artfully under the man, thinking too much. Hoping. Deflating. You wonder if W, too, always has a notebook close.

~

Growing up, your mother wouldn't allow you to even countenance the idea of being a writer. It was too risky, flighty, unknown. She'd drilled into you various mantras for womanhood to guide you through life. Buy your own property. Get on the mortgage ladder as soon as you can. Never sign over your property to a man, or even half of it, if it had been acquired before your relationship. When she died several decades beyond this time she owned her own flat outright, which she'd bought for herself post divorce, and had a healthy superannuation pot. Your father, in contrast, lived his last years in penury after decades of financially reckless living and the disintegration of his second marriage. You realise belatedly how magnificent and empowered your mother was yet gave her no credit for her lessons observed when she was alive; you never said thank you for everything you absorbed.

Do women ever express gratitude, enough, to their mothers? Why are we so hard on them? Sylvia Plath's mother told her an English major who knew shorthand would be so much more desirable than a 'plain English major'. According to her mother, Plath wrote in *The Bell Jar*, 'Everybody would want her. She would be in demand among all the up-and-coming young men and she would transcribe letter after thrilling letter.' The problem was, Plath said, 'I hated the idea of serving men in any way. I wanted to dictate my own thrilling letters.'

You couldn't tell W, during all the writing talk in the ute, that you wanted to *be* interviewed eventually – not spend your life interviewing someone else. Your mother dreamed of you being on television, and if you were to insist on a career in journalism then being on the box was an acceptable choice for her daughter. She pushed and prodded you to be TV ambitious yet you had no hunger. Your mother was contemptuous about writing. To her it meant starving in fingerless gloves in an attic.

She was afraid of you writing. Of what the words might reveal lying behind the carefully constructed façade she had constructed for herself, a world of cultural refinement with rounded vowels and a season subscription to the Australian ballet. For in the grand ballroom of destiny reversal your mother reigned supreme. She was also afraid of the poverty writing would invariably trap her daughter into. You had brushed up too close to the have-nots in life. She wasn't convinced that a world of books would be any kind of evolution. In her thinking, the people who wrote were the people who could afford to write. You couldn't. There was an indulgent luxury to it, a dilettantish expansiveness that you had no right to partake of. You were something different – a worker.

~

Your mother saw who W was from the moment of meeting him. Perceived instantly that he existed in a tenuous world of share houses and teenage attire into his thirties, where no one owned a car or knew the intricacies of bank loans. To her he smelt of the student world, one that hadn't quite crossed the divide into responsible adulthood. She was afraid of what it would bind you to. She wanted her daughter free and stable and financially secure and she perceived it would take a regular job to buy that freedom because decades of hard work had taught her this. You were learning that writers are the risk takers, that all artists are, but it's not always appreciated by those around them.

~

Deep into the night W and you talk of the anonymity of places that are not home. Because you can be anyone there, don't have to be that person you're expected to be, the conformist among the tight circles you've grown up in. You tell W of the women who meekly fall into line in the suburbia you come from; their safe, small lives they never question. Who is the happier, you wonder aloud. Those who stay or those who escape? Those content with their lot or those who hungrily want something more, something else?

They're censorious of people like you. Your choices aren't celebrated; there's no curiosity among old school friends about your new life, your new worlds.

'I wanted to be where nobody I knew could ever come,' Sylvia Plath wrote in *The Bell Jar* and you know exactly what she meant. The exhilaration of anonymity will always lure you, because within it you can find the freedom to be your true self. To live a self-determined life, without judgement.

~

You do not tell W you crave love, and that this craving is perhaps coloured by the fact many of your old school friends are settling into long-term relationships now. The pattern for many of the girls is to go to university and live at home until an engagement a few years later, then get married in their mid-twenties and embark on motherhood, which brings a swift end to their working life. It feels so old-fashioned, predictable, safe, and you're the outlier among it. These women seem to acquire partners from their world easily, in lives enveloped by solid families that are never touched by divorce or money worries or trauma. They feel like they're from another world, one where they wouldn't dream of retaining their surname upon marrying. They'd move one or two suburbs away from childhood homes and their children would be expected to follow suit in a pattern replicated through generations of safe, narrow, comfortable existences. The expectations of this future tighten around you as the years progress. Suffocate you. Because you know you are different.

Which is why you're now living in Alice Springs and not among those good Catholic women from the homes of doctors and barristers. They feel almost like prisoners to you, victims of a Stockholm syndrome of a small life. Because the world has gaslighted you all into thinking that this is the best way to be, for a young woman, a model of excellence you should all aspire to. You don't buy it but the women around you do, and judge, and find you wanting. There's a whiff of selfishness in your wanting to hold out for a unique, free, blazing life.

Meanwhile a malignity coils in you and waits. It's a ferocious desire to live a singular life. Slowly, steadily, silently it pulses as you fill up journal after journal, and watch.

9

The owner of the Nevertire pub reaches a strong hand from behind the bar, searching out names and setting them in concrete. W and you prop your elbows simultaneously on the counter, flagging. W asks for a room. 'What? Twin beds?' the pub owner exclaims. You both nod. He grins like a knowing elder brother.

The two of you unpack the back of the ute, at W's suggestion. You're working together, he's looking out for you, it's what you've always wanted. Bob Dylan is on the tape deck, you go inside to order drinks, the boys at the bar ask you to sit by them while 'your boyfriend' is outside. 'He's not my boyfriend,' you snap but smile inside. Then W and you play pool with a cotton picker and his girlfriend and you're not too bad, thanks to endless days whittling away boredom in your grandfather's pool room. But you're fading fast. You shower then head back to the bedroom that can't be locked.

W is in the narrow single bed next to you, reading Dostoyevsky's *The Idiot*. You slip into the bed beside his. A small table divides you. So. Here you are, side by side in narrow, saggy, school camp beds. You tire together. 'He snores, I don't mind,' you write later in your journal. You would mind, usually, but the idea of him is leaking into you. The thought of life with him, a possible future.

~

How often does a man's snoring crash into a woman's sanity and serenity? Her creativity? How often does she bear it by sacrificing her own comfort? You don't care back then because you're falling; W is the embodiment of everything you've ever wanted and you willingly surrender. It's the embodiment of the concept of 'Writer'. And because he's actually living it there's a humbleness to him, a self-deprecating wryness. And in his presence you want to be erased. To have him, to have everything you've dreamed of. You want the great annihilation.

This is a story of rebirth.

~

You have set out on this road trip wearing RM Williams boots with the toe section re-leathered and jodhpurs and snug little tees and a slim, worn Akubra hat because you've lived for three years already in the Northern Territory. And every couple of days since the age of thirteen you've shaved your legs and underarms for whoever will never see them. You think yourself fat; not blessed in terms of attractiveness. Yet looking back on photos from this era you're slim, shining, ripe, in the glorious prime of woman-hood yet unable to recognise it. It's all about confidence, of course. Confidence is sexy, it lightens you. Why do you loathe yourself so much? Who planted that seed? The world, you suspect.

~

W, with his paperback now facedown on the table that divides you, feels like your everything on this night. You're ripe for a rescuing, all desire. You know passion, grand passion, only through books. Cathy and Heathcliff, Heliose and Abelard, Jane Eyre and Rochester, Anna Karenina and Vronsky. You're trigger-ready tonight. Have always been very particular. Know instantly with every man – yes or no – and most often it's a definite no. But with W, next to you in his bed, you're all focused want.

~

Why do so few men around you fall into the category of Object of Desire? Are all women as picky? Your tastes are wilfully obscure. And it's always been unrequited. The handful of one-night stands you have slept with have never been objects of lust, they were experiments. You were watching, noting, accumulating, refining. Detached.

All the questions. Why did it hurt? Why were you not enjoying it? Why was it so monotonous as they thrusted?

Why did you never want it to go on for too long? Why did the big penises hurt when they were meant to be the coveted ones? Why did you feel deadened under them? Why did it feel humiliating when they came over your face then spread it across your skin and through your hair, sometimes rubbing it in for good measure; what imperative of ownership and erasure was going on there? As if you were not quite human, not thinking, reeling, blazing, bewildered you.

Years later a lover twenty years older explained he lost interest in women as they neared thirty. Why? But you knew, without even asking the question. Because by thirty women know too much. They're aware. And that's a gift and a burden, because it's not what the insecure man wants.

~

You know on this Nevertire night you would be happy to not mention your writing dream, ever; you would reduce yourself that much. To have this man. So as not to appear better, stronger, smarter, somehow above the one who's the object of your desire. To not scare him off. Because you have learnt.

~

Yet why are you so keen on the narrative of surrender when it comes to love? With the falling, the falling under, why are you spelled? Is it biology? The urges of a submissive, baby-ready body? You hate this want within you to pair up with someone, yet crave it. How odd you are in this moment, in this hotel room, so emptied and waiting to be filled. By another. A lifetime of telling you you're wrong in some way is what does it, perhaps. Wrong to think the way you do, wrong to want to be a writer, wrong to want a career beyond the confines of suburbia, wrong to be competitive and driven. It feels like a process of silencing. Yet you do not want the cautious, meek, quiet life expected of you, because that will not be an authentic life.

~

W is a study of carefully curated literary cool, and poverty; everything your mother would be horrified by in a future son-in-law. So of course it has to be him. To break from her. If a child of your parents has the brains they will do law or medicine, surely. To climb out, to astonish. They would never become – horror – a writer. 'Waste of time, that,' was your father's instant, chuckly dismissal when you told him in your early twenties that you wanted to write novels one day.

Yet if the right man comes along you will readily move from your beloved Alice Springs, you will wrench yourself from the place that repairs you from the toss of life. You'll head back to Sydney if you must, the hometown that feels so narrow and judgemental and known. For love. But it will take someone very special for that. Someone in sync with you and your singular ways – and you've wondered increasingly if they can ever be found. And now this.

10

The ping of his digital watch wakes you at 5.45 am. He means business. It's your kind of energy. You both wallop down bacon and eggs at a truck-stop café. The waitress talks casually about Alice Springs being 'lousy with Aboriginals' and you both recoil at the shock of the open racism. Then relax into the driving and push the car strong into the wide open space. The sky expands before you as the ground flattens around you. You're confident now with the mechanism of the gears, chasing the shadows of the clouds just ahead of you, laughing and holding your hand high out the window, butting the breeze.

You take photos, urgently, to capture the momentum of these heady days; of hesitant companionship, of falling. Even if this man – *man* – never becomes your boyfriend you can stick the black-and-white shots on the wall of some future bedroom and remember. He is no boy. The rest were. Hurting and careless and unaware, confident and arrogant. This one has lived enough to grow humble. He feels like an intellectual match. He'll not crowd you out, who you really are, he'll give you space for that.

How fragile and brave and deluded and silly you are and barely know it. Except perhaps you do, deep down, but can barely admit it; that this isn't exactly, openly you beside this man in your ute. Something is stealing your strength. Who you really are. In the rush to re-make yourself you're forgetting the steady, focused path to some kind of success. Because you perceive this man mightn't want a driven type of girl, so soon, it might scare him off. You scrawl in your journal that if you had the chance to have a novel published, or a passionate love, you'd choose the latter no question.

Enthusiasm comes from the Greek, *enthousiasmos*, meaning 'inspiration or possession by a god', or 'spark of God'. Before W you had enthusiasm for writing; with W, you have enthusiasm for love. And the two feel mutually exclusive.

~

Talk on the open road is of Bob Dylan and Nick Cave and Wim Wenders and Michael Ondaatje; his favourite creatives. He speaks of relationships, how elusive they are for him. Tells you he was asked to be a priest at school and that God and his belief are strong. You gulp all the talk and think you begin to love right here. Looking back you want to be very tender with this young woman who has no idea as she falls for a man going on and on about Dylan – a singer you've never liked, although you won't admit it. Looking back, so tender, because of all the changes, all the little inauthentic adjustments you're going through with him. 'You have to be very fond of men. Very, very fond,' Marguerite Duras wrote in *Practicalities*. 'You have to be very fond of them to love them. Otherwise they're simply unbearable.' And you were.

In the ute on the highway you will toss the writing dream away to fuck this man and keep fucking him, the sexual urge is that strong. Do men ever experience that annihilation, or are they too ruthless?

~

A pit stop at Silverton, a parched, outback town. You both saunter into the cool of the only pub. All its clientele sit around a large square counter and stare, as one, ahead. There's a long cool hush as if there's no use wasting energy on all that bustle of talk, as if anything worth talking about has been exhausted long ago. The dog lying outside the door has 'No Food' spray-painted blue on its back, warning you off. And you're all a-churn. Because something is morphing between W and you, in your groin.

On you drive and on, pushing the faithful ute over a strange rise in the middle of nowhere with a train track underneath it like a child's plastic toy on a lounge room floor. You stop and get out and both walk the empty tracks, feeling dangerous and daring and alone in the world like the kids in *The Railway Children*. Sky horses are wild in the clouds. He stands beside you, nudges, you lean in, stop. Tension. You push on to another pit stop for a twilight drink and the kid behind the bar laps W up – the clothes, hair; hunger for the city, any city, in his eyes. W and you sit side by side on the verandah outside. There's a companionable silence that isn't awkward and you wonder if that's the secret to a good relationship, that you can be comfortable in silence. W talks of the ranger at Jabiru and the letter he wrote to the girl he loved six years ago, and never sent. 'Oh, missed lives!' you exclaim and tell him you never want to be like that. Because life is about risking, surely. Picking yourself up after failure, persisting. He nods. Gets it. You smile. He smiles back. Tension.

~

You push on to Orroroo, a town neither of you knows how to say. There's no room at the inn at the first place, the second is fifty bucks. 'Only twin beds I'm afraid.' 'That's okay,' hurried, in unison. You feel charged, together in your room, both flat on your backs on your respective beds, talking of books and poetry and music. W says he wants to take you out for a drink one day, to get you in context, see you in the real world, know you; for this is anything but a normal introduction. Yes, you nod, yes. You wake together at 3.30 am with him murmuring something about 'Mr and Mrs Gemmell' that the lady at the counter had checked you in as; he's musing over it, softly chuckling in the black, 'I like it.' Your belly trembles, you do too.

Later, wide awake in the close dark, you think of Sylvia Plath who wrote to her mother when she first met Ted Hughes, explaining that he was the only man who she felt would be strong enough for her to be equal with. Yet within a year of meeting him Plath was typing up his poems and sending them off to a literary competition in the US, which she'd found out about for herself. It was a competition for a first book of poetry and the illustrious judges – Marianne Moore, WH Auden and Stephen Spender – awarded Hughes first prize for *The Hawk in the Rain*, which was subsequently published as Hughes's debut volume. He felt guilty that it was his poems and not his girlfriend's that were to be published, yet Plath publicly rejoiced. Told her mother that Hughes would be ahead of her now but there was no question of rivalry; only a mutual joy and a sense of them doubling the prize-winning and creative output. Would that one day be W and you, you wondered. No sense of rivalry, but mutual joy, the dream.

～

Over breakfast W talks about how he wants to be 'the cool dad'. Talks about family and history. You push on into salt pan country and stop in the vast emptiness and jump outside and howl together on an endless expanse of salt pan, wind-whipped. It's exhilarating, you want to kiss, he stares for a second or two too long. A storm is gathering up ahead. You keep going. To beat it.

The sky is plummeting to earth. A shower curtain, grey, is drawn across the length of the horizon and you stop the car again and get out into pummelling rain and the intoxicating smell of the earth opening up to receive its benediction. 'It's King Lear!' You laugh as the wind flurries around you and W laughs too, knowing exactly what you mean. He's looking at you, you want to kiss, feel wet, your body taking over. Snap away. You get back in the car and drive on under angry splots and you're suddenly into the weather furious. You yank down the window and put out your hand like a dog, hold out your palm to the sting of the wet and W does the same and you feel electric, wild, then drive out of it suddenly into silly happy sun-spot rain, pinging from the windshield in a joyous dance. And all around you is that heady smell of the world opening up; the thirsty earth expanding, waking, exploding.

You head into darkness to camp somewhere by the side of the road; there are no towns left. A kamikaze bird slams into the windscreen. 'Fuck!' you exclaim. W chuckles in an affectionate tease, he won't say a word. The hot outside is pressing in and suddenly he's pouring water into his hands and trickling it silently over your forehead as you drive and it slips down your chin, cold between your breasts, then to your belly as you push the ute on and on and he does it again, and again, and pours it into your hands as you keep your eyes on the road and rub your neck and stretch behind the wheel and think, electric and earthy and strong, think. That you could get used to this. Wet.

~

A pit stop for food, sausages and bread. After a drench under a tap you listen to a policeman's advice on where the best camping spot is. You drive on and arrive at the suggested creek, make the turn to the dirt, to the creek bed. The sand is white and virgin and soft, you drive a little further, a little further, and . . . sink. The ute stops. Oh no, God no. Well and truly bogged. In the middle of nowhere.

You know what to do. In the Northern Territory you've tackled numerous bogs; W, you suspect, has no idea. You feel strong with experience and get down into the sand and dig, clawing the dirt. His beautiful artist's hands are side by side with yours, panicking, scooping. You go back to the driver's seat and rev and return to the digging. Nothing works. You jump in the tray of the ute and rip open a box that holds your city books and tear up the cardboard and place it under the ute's wheels and try again and again with the revving and move, just, and try again, and dig, and again. Your energy is drained then W thinks to unpack the back of the ute to lighten it; of course! But no. You stumble onto the empty highway and wander it like two accident victims. The road is empty. You walk along the edge of the bitumen, cloaked in silence and worry. You see a lone truckie pulled over up ahead, settling down for evening chops. You – the ferals – stumble over to a man ludicrously clean and neat. His CB radio can't do the trick because you're all too far from anywhere and he'd never get his rig into the creek but he promises to tell the cops as he goes through the next town which is too far to walk to.

You set up camp, you'll tackle it all in the morning. After a dinner of baked beans and snags and unbearable tension you settle into swags and silence and watch the lightning show silently far away in the sky, like an orchestra here, now there, and together. Somewhere in the darkness, softly W says, 'I think this has been the best day of my life,' and he brushes your hand, brotherly, what, you don't know, don't respond. Oh no, have you lost this forever, please no. You're shy, hesitant, not sure of what he means yet feel unbearably close to him. He rubs your shoulder and again you don't respond, not knowing. Can't act. Seized up. Unsure. W sinks away. Silence. He draws across the flap of his swag and you cannot read his goodnight. You settle. This has to be done. As you say goodnight you reach across and rub his wrist and he rubs strongly back.

It is done.

~

Joy is roguish through you. You have become a howl. Then, in the middle of it, you realise the cold and the lightning is upon you and there's a mad naked scrabble to the ute. The swags are thrown in its back and a tarp pulled over; everything else is snug in the cabin or crammed in the corners of the tray and your bodies will just have to fit.

And just before you crawl inside you stand with W's arm around your shoulder and stare in silence at the wind and lightning and vast clouds crowding above you and feel strong together, like some couple from an earlier time who've been through epic, wringing things.

You both crawl into the tray of the ute, inside the sliver of space, under the tarpaulin. 'This is something to tell the great-grandchildren.' W chuckles and you hold each other while the rain thunders above you. He is wet, all his back, then you're wet, your face, as the wily rain wends its way inside but you're holding tight. And in the rain gaps you clamber-crawl into a sitting position and poke your heads out of the tarp and stare at the lightning dancing in the sky then sink into the close darkness and you eat the sweat and the dirt off his skin and sleep is snatched, somewhere, pre-dawn. And you now know you will throw everything else away – all focus, grit, ambition – for this. To say it is yours. At last.

~

During this trip you are reading Doris Lessing, her auto-biographical book, *Walking in the Shade*. Lessing described how she was afraid to tell her lover, Jack, that she had won an award for young writers, the Somerset Maugham Prize. When she did tell him, Jack exclaimed, '"And that's it, that's the end."' Lessing observed, 'It came from his depths, from his deep, dark male depths . . . "You don't love me; you only care about your writing."' From Jack's unhappy outburst Lessing concluded that there was probably not one woman writer, ever, who had not heard something like this from her man.

~

All around you, as you devour the words of the female writers you constantly read, are little warning signs, yet you do not heed them. You vaguely sense you need to find the gift of a man unthreatened by your vocation. You need to find the gift of a man who will let you be free, to do what you really want to in life.

But right now you are tumbling into the vastness of a swamping, consuming passion. There is the language of diminishment to accompany it: a falling, a surrendering, a loss of self. There is the willing violation of the clear, hard, glittery core of who you really are, who you lose on this night. But you don't care. Because you have in your grasp now what you've always wanted.

Love.

11

A sullen dawn. A strong kiss. Your lips are worn from the scratch of W's stubble, your skin torn. He pulls you to him and you feel his hardness and succumb then both stumble onto the highway, the two ferals, mud-encrusted and sex-encrusted. His shirt is off and you're grubby and damp and a four-wheel drive pulls over at your mad waving, and what do you know? The driver turns out to be a professional towing expert who has an enormous blue tow rope for coaches stuck in Top End bogs. Your ute slips from the sand, demure.

W and you babble thanks and you grab some fancy Sydney chocolates, which you'd bought for your Alice Springs newsroom colleagues, and give them to your rescuer then drive silly-happy onto the highway and stop, and kiss, again. You take a photo of this elemental, tell-the-grandchildren spot. W tells you that his relationships have always been a quest to find a marriage of the intellectual, the physical and the spiritual and then he looks at you and smiles and you smile back and begin to love, deeply. Then back on the road you stop once more and kiss and almost fuck into the side of the car in the emptiness of not another soul, anywhere, the emptiness of just the two of you in a wide ringing world. Then it's back to the highway with your hand strong on his thigh and your cheeks suddenly soft together, celebrating the pull of whatever astonishment has just happened between you.

~

You stop at the Olgas, Kata Tjuta. Lie in the sun by yourself then hear the scrunch of his boots and you bury your face into his thigh and soak him up and wish there weren't tourists all around because you want to fuck him, right here by the path; this is making you careless and reckless and you walk back to the ute, holding, pushing, basking, wondrous. At this force between you.

He talks about kids, how he wants to be the cool dad marching around the house with three of them trailing behind him; he's got it all pictured. Where is the woman in that snapshot, you wonder fleetingly, but stronger than that you're thinking, *These are* my *kids he's imagining,* this *is why he's saying it.* You laugh at the image and record it later in your journal and only years later read it as a ploy to draw you in, his talking kids and marriage and togetherness so fast. But there's no cynicism right now, it's pure want; your body is taking over your life with a new subservience.

~

As a writer, you sense you have one thing that will stand you in good stead, more than any talent you might have in the job. Grit.

You studied creative writing at university, within a general journalism degree at undergraduate level and then exclusively for an MA. Both degrees involved small, tightknit groups of writers who would workshop their prose on a weekly basis. Amid the handful of high hopefuls were some writers who would turn out perfectly formed paragraphs of brilliant prose, and how you envied them. Yet you had an inkling even back then that those snippets of writerly perfection would never amount to the dream of a published book. Why? Because their creators didn't have the will and stamina to see it through.

Yet how to marry the drive and hunger and focus with love and babies, with the swamping of domesticity? You want it all and it feels impossible. It frightens you.

~

You sail into Alice Springs, floating on a high of all that has happened on this road trip into a new existence. You pull the ute over and climb a ridge and look at the town stretched ahead. W comes up beside you and tells you he will take you out to dinner next week in Alice. All his friends in this place, well, they're at the top of his list, he has to be with them and you must remember that.

Sea anemone, you close in on yourself, and continue into Alice Springs with a silence, weighty and rich, between you. Brimful of anger, desolation, unrequited love, and loss.

~

That night you scribble in your journal wild words. That your strength and stamina do not depend on another and you must never succumb, you will not be chipped away, you're too strong for that. Surely. When you are your blazing self, settled and ready, you will choose another to enhance your world, but only when you're ready. And not now, not yet. But you're all soft underbelly in your lone bed, curling in the sheets amid the bleakness of rejection, drawing the doona over your head.

~

W explains, a week or so later, that you misheard him or it came out awkwardly or wrong but he meant to say it was you, actually, who's at the top of his list and it takes you both seven days to chance upon this mad mishear that almost destroys what you had. And by then W has already said he loves you when you're nodding off to sleep beside him with your loose hand resting across his sharp, Jesus hip. And he says in one of the long, laugh-saturated bed raves that it's like you were both married out there, by the elements, the land and storm and sky and air. He declares that if you'd both stayed on the road a week longer you would've been married on the Tuesday, having kids on the Wednesday and in your graves by the Saturday. It was that intense.

You had always thought of yourself as a girl and you tell him this and he responds, 'I think I've found the woman in you.' Yet deep down you feel like you're a lover; still not entirely a woman. Because to you a woman is strong, her own person, fierce and free; blunt with her words and saying no to so much. To you a woman is not bound by love, but freed by it. But that knowledge will only come to you many years later.

12

'Distracted, distracted, deliciously distracted,' you write in your journal of this time when your heart is flooded, because you're getting no proper writing done, because this is not what this time is for.

Male creativity feels like power. You're in awe of W's craft. Subservient to it, willing to be silent and accommodating and helpful for it. Your own creativity is softening in the face of his. You can feel the lessening of your own intent, little acquiescences, again and again. You will write next month, next year. You feel empowered by love amid all of W's attention, tall and strong and buoyed by a new confidence. It is enough. Nothing else matters. You are changed.

W retains something of himself, his writing self, ruthlessly. This is the fundamental difference in the relationship. He still works with focus, comfortably retaining his chip of ice that guiltlessly removes him from regular life; you're aware his creative world takes precedence over yours and do not question this. Meanwhile you're busy dreaming of weddings and pregnancies, of kids brimming a giggle palace of a house. As Elizabeth Hardwick wrote, biology is destiny – but only for girls. Yet amid it all you feel the small, hard blade of a chilly truth: that the ultimate commitment, perhaps, is to be a female writer attached to a male writer. And right now you're ready to throw yourself away for it.

~

W has come to Alice to write a story. As a journalist already based in the town you help him with contacts and research. You think of Charmian Clift and the sense of release she was referring to when she declared she was sick of being the 'literary hod-carrier' to her husband, George Johnston. Clift used this expression to explain the end of her novel-writing collaborations between herself and Johnston, and after that she bloomed as a novelist and columnist in her own right.

~

It feels, during this time with W, that you want to know life instead of guessing at it; you want to know a deep, passionate love at last. Your head is full of images to send you into sleep every night. Breaking open a church at midnight to get married by moonlight, passing a ring between lips, a wide bed draped with children. And all through this, like a dragging anchor, is the dullness of your reporting job as opposed to love's wild allure. But love is killing the writing urge. You're learning that happiness is growing you soft and complacent yet you don't care. You give in, float, succumb.

~

W and you settle into a partnered life – you in Alice Springs, he in Sydney – with regular flying visits. In the early months of the arrangement, on the Alice sojourns, there's his boy-mad rushing out to say goodbye on your work mornings, both a little unsure of how to do this level of intensely partnered domesticity. There are laughing, meandering chats and fucks and sleeps when you come home from work early in the afternoon after a morning shift and lie together and kiss and giggle in your low futon bed on its polished concrete floor the colour of the Uluru earth. There's the way, soft-strong, almost as a chant, W commands, 'Take it out,' of your tampon before fucking you through the blood. You're like newlyweds at a bush restaurant far out of town and later in a little honeymoon cabin next to it. And at an airport farewell you sit in stillness, cheek to cheek, in nondescript plastic chairs then you write in your journal straight after the leaving, 'unbearable pull, last desperate kiss, tears inside, want, blind want'. You feel taken over. By love. By desire. Arrowed to W at the expense of your own life. Back in Sydney he writes that every conversation sneaks inspiration upon him and he just wants to be with you forever, complete and strong; with you, his soul mate, his elemental wife. You press his letter to your chest as if to shield the urgency of the words from the rest of the world. You feel empowered by his love and shy and wondrous with it.

~

Now it's your turn to visit Sydney. He drives you to his home from the airport; he's borrowed a car from a mate. You connect at once and as you roam his pianist's hands he murmurs, 'You feel beautiful.' His dreamed-of garret room is exuberant with books and magazines and aesthetics and you sit at his tall attic window, late into the night, staring out into the rain-bright evening, flush with love and life and feeling strongly that there are new worlds ahead for you now, as a woman, at last.

Your father's words on your birthday card resonate. 'I release you to your destiny.' He's pleased, proud, as if his oddball, misunderstood daughter is growing up at last. Perhaps this deeply conservative coalminer understands something you don't; he sees a domestic life opening up for you and is pleased, because he'd always expected this of the women in his life, through two marriages and seven kids. Perhaps he sees the generational patterns being cemented now and is pleased that his perplexing, singular, untameable daughter is being tamed, at last.

~

W bites your flesh in lovemaking, he bruises you as if he wants to brand you forever. You let him without thinking anything of it: this is Passion, yes? You wear his love-made thumb prints, green and purple clouds against the pale sky of your skin. You breathe him in like a first cigarette. His fingers slip inside your underpants and you feel your insides peel away and your groin softly contract, and buck, and open out like a flower to his palm, offering wetness.

Lying in bed, in a soft morning, he murmurs that he can see you both in Grandma's feather bed with some kids between you and you glow within. Heading into the country by train, to visit both your families, you stare out at humble little bush cottages across the Hawkesbury River as he speculates that it'd be a good place to bring up kids, and you embrace and his squeeze tells you there are worlds ahead, together, and you are charged, reeled in, lit.

In Sydney's airport café, about to head back to Alice, W says that he really wants this to last and you reply, 'I want to have your children,' and he gives you a squeeze of yes, yes. Bugger the writing life.

~

Back in Alice, in a tougher world, the demanding heat pushes into you. 'I haven't heard from him for several days,' you write tetchily in your journal, 'he could run me off the rails.' A dust storm skips across Alice and the sky turns an eery, ferocious pink and it's apocalyptic, otherworldly and you feel febrile and unnerved as you wait. For what? 'She had lived her early years as though she were waiting for something she might, but never did, become,'

Marguerite Duras wrote in *The Ravishing of Lol Stein*. The whisper of the pull of those words, as you sense in these low times that you're becoming someone else amid the unthinking happiness of true love, whatever that is. Yet does W realise the damage he's doing by not contacting you? Does he understand the carelessness – for that's what it feels like – when you're held hostage to his silence? Does he even realise the damage he's doing to your psyche when you're unable to think of anything else? When he doesn't call, doesn't give any affirmation, doesn't reach out across the void. It is the piracy of indifference and all your strength is sapped. W has the ability to make you feel small. Lesser, needy, submissive. It's a dangerous power. You hope he respects it. You feel smaller than you've ever felt before; and you're willing to go even smaller. He is faltering you.

~

He rings at last. There's love, laughter, wetness, want, instantly of course. Everything else is forgotten in the communion of him. You think back to the first night together in your Alice Springs house, of falling softly to sleep while facing each other with your hand cupped to his chest and it was a communication, but more, a communion. That word of grace, spiritually softened, and amid it all is forgotten, forgiven.

~

Over the long months apart from each other you work on becoming the woman you think he wants; the image of a cool, inner-city rocker chick in your head. Skinny, care-free, out of the ordinary and effortlessly wearing vintage. You lose weight. Drape yourself in new clothes. A friend tells you he is disappearing you, that you're vanishing. It gives you pause. You conclude she's jealous and press on.

~

You've been going out for three months now, passing the first milestone of an enduring relationship. On the unsatisfactory telephone, to mark the occasion, he tells you he got soaked in the rain walking home the previous night and it was wonderful and elemental all at once and he was crying out your name and all afternoon you're drenched with him, wet and wanting.

~

In fiction you can see the clear path of where this is going, yet in real life can't. You refuse to think of a likely ending, you exist in the present with this. Could never be truthful about this man, in your heart, because you love him too much. Are in love with him too much. Are in love with love too much. And because of this you don't see him.

13

Christmas. With a group of scientists, specialists in desert landscapes and climate and endangered mammals. Good people who know how to party, earnest and smart. They've found a waterhole off the beaten tourist track, west of town, and this is to be your yuletide destination. On Christmas Eve ten of you load up a handful of four-wheel drives with swags, bush ovens, cocktail shakers, tins of tea and tinsel for the anointed bush pine. You're all without family out here, childless and Godless. The land is your cathedral and none of you wish for anything else.

Bush tracks falter, lose their will and almost peter out. After several bone-jolting hours in the utes you arrive by a stunningly beautiful waterhole and select the appropriate pine for a trussing with all the solemnity of ceremony. Then climb a nearby bluff and drink margaritas under a sunset that seems as wide as heaven itself. Your bush Christmas has begun. It will last for several days and you all feel daring and exclusive, modern and defiant, stranded from family, from regular life.

This festive ritual feels a blessed world away from all the ghosts of Christmases past. Childhood ceremonies of tepid turkeys with too many family members crammed into airless, sweltering lounge rooms. And after divorce fractured everything there was the complication of allegiances where you had to travel from gathering to gathering, to aging relatives from opposing factions who hugged you too tight and cooed identical 'my haven't you grown's. These are people who were once great friends yet never speak to each other anymore. As a child it was all too bewildering. As you grow older the split-family shunting and sweltering lounge rooms never change, but the questions do. 'When are you going to settle down, love?' Yes, you do have a boyfriend, finally. And yes you are happy, finally. But you don't need to tell your family this in person, yet; it is as if something in your bones tells you it's not quite set, yet.

Out bush, happiness brims you. Friends are the new family and you've chosen this lot. Like-minded people, cloistered by a shared desire to be Elsewhere. You're all from somewhere far away and all secretly relieved to be removed from the hooks of family obligation. Presents home have been sent weeks ago, you're now free and alone and it's bliss. It feels, to you, like a final hurrah to singledom.

~

Back to reality. Shiftwork. You sink into routine and socialising in your tight little desert town that feels so removed from anywhere else. You attend a dinner party with other journalists that's competitive and loud and shouty, soaked in performance. You wander outside two or three times during the evening to gulp the clean night air, alone, to gulp space and silence, wanting the calmness of W very much. He is cloaking you in want, removing you from everything else. He tells you later that he had to cover the last letter from you with his hand; he loved it so much. It was a letter about something being decided between you and passionate journeys and a rare, enduring love and you shudder deep in your bowels as he talks.

~

You had always been wary of men and their confidence but felt you needed them back then, to complete your life. Felt, tuggingly, the bindings of womanhood; the want, the need for them when you were most ripe. You didn't feel complete without them, yet weaker with them, and that was an intriguing dilemma of life.

~

An earlier boyfriend, A, taught you to be comfortable with your body; W, to love your body. What it could do, and what a gift that was. The realisation of what your body was capable of. Without these men you never would have learnt the secrets to unlocking your body. You could've easily gone through life faking orgasms and pretending enjoyment and no one would have been any the wiser. Your grandmother told you that she had never enjoyed sex, and that could have so easily been you.

~

W writes that he's fallen in love with your soul, his feelings are that strong. That he's with you, always. At this stage you've fallen headlong in love with your life choice as opposed to your work choice. There is no contest. Yet you had always been Yeats's 'world besotted traveller', until this man; curiosity was your propellant, until him.

He's never left the country. You've been on many trips by the time he comes into your life. Any money you make goes towards your next adventure; that's the pattern of your saving. By your mid-twenties you've already had two of what the travel industry calls a 'round the world ticket'. But all this experience counts for nothing with W, he isn't interested in where you've been. He always seems more during this time, more than what you could ever offer. You, less. He makes you feel that your experience with the Other – other skies, countries, ways – is irrelevant to what you have together.

~

A few months into your relationship with W, you travel to Cuba and Jamaica with your mother, a trip a year in the planning. But to W it could have been anywhere, he's not interested. Is it that he doesn't want you to have a life that's bigger and better than his in some way, you wonder. This feels like pirate love suddenly. Taking, plundering, and you're willingly giving yourself up to it.

You feel for the first time you could be hurt into writing by his actions. That he's giving you the taste of a very lonely life. You wonder if it's worth it, for W is making you fear disturbance. Making you cautious. He's quelling your restlessness and curiosity as you contemplate a quieter domestic life. Yet curiosity has always been fuel for you, writing fuel. Anger has always felt good to you. It gets things done.

~

Anger. A much maligned word, especially when it comes to women. Historically we're not meant to question. To be explosive and loud and stroppy and furious. Yet many of us are, about so much. Anger is a force for change and when you see it in a female who has been wronged or talked over or drowned out it can feel magnificent. Releasing. Clarifying. Because the sharp-shod hoof of fury strikes the soft underbelly of complacency and changes the world. Slowly. And the collective harnessing of anger at certain historical moments feels necessary. It's an outlet, a corrective.

Anger changes a world dictated to us by others, a world meant to keep us in our place. For women, that place is a very quiet, unquestioning, removed existence. Anger barges us to a seat at the table, to spaces we're traditionally not invited to or only reluctantly. Anger that transforms, shifting the culture in some way, usually begins with a cry of unfairness that connects all the wounded psyches.

Women are always being told to not be angry. That it's unbecoming, unfeminine, unnecessary. *Calm down, dear. Get back to your kitchen. Stop screeching.* Yet how else are we to bring about change if not through anger? How else are we to blaze a more equal world? Every week you see the forces of the silencing banking up against women who have a voice in the media or politics or letters. The aim: to meeken. To vanish their uncomfortable truths.

Yet anger is the emotion of self-regard and self-worth. It's a cry to the world that you deserve better, a cry of the person wronged. A launch pad to self-esteem. Anger towards men who treat women appallingly is changing our world for the better. Women pay the price for male insecurity again and again and we must never stop calling it out. Our voice – our angry one – is a weapon for change. Russian poet Anna Akhmatova wrote once, so powerfully, that we would remember her when we heard thunder; we would remember how she had wanted storms. Because storms cleanse.

~

W says he almost feels sick when you leave to go overseas to Cuba. During your trip with your mother the thought of marriage and a quieter domestic life makes you feel lonely. Cut off. Marooned. From who you really are, and from your writing life. On the day of your return, back in Sydney, W whispers, 'I want you to be my woman forever,' when he's deep inside you. 'I feel you're a part of me,' he whispers, roping you in tighter.

~

Others can see the likely future for you with W, but you are blind to their reasoning. Your best friend from school and your mother try to warn you of the life ahead with a man in his thirties who's never been overseas and still rents and doesn't have a car and only loosely adheres to the concept of deadlines, despite being a freelance writer albeit a stunning one; he exists as 'the creative genius' – such a male construct in itself. You know you can't change him and don't want to. You're after a story, a legend, rather than an actual person. W is almost a figment of your imagination, for you've longed for this type of person, this relationship, for so long.

~

You've always been competitive. Driven. Want to succeed intellectually and never want your writer lover's success to eclipse your own. They never know this but it's the secret truth. Yet, as Toni Morrison said, for a woman to say *I am a writer*, well, it's difficult. And now, oddly, you are supine when it comes to ambition when once you wanted it so much. Yet a desire to succeed curls in you and waits, like a cold, watchful cat.

14

Great female creators – the like of Artemisia Gentileschi, Camille Claudel, Virginia Woolf and Sylvia Plath to name a few – lived audaciously and with great courage; they preserved a sense of difference despite strong headwinds. All were mavericks. Women are expected to conform to society's expectations of what they should be, yet many of our successful female artists' modus operandi is about breaking down rigid societal bindings.

You become fascinated during this time with the idea of the artist's muse. With the male artist who expects obedience from his female partner, that quasi-servant, assistant, cook, fuck. The word muse implies obedience and submission, a softening of one's own raging will to another. Yet obedience is one thing a female artist should not be good at. She should be audacious, needs to fail at obedience to succeed. 'I didn't have time to be anyone's muse,' the British–Mexican painter and writer Leonora

Carrington declared. 'I was too busy rebelling . . . and learning to be an artist.'

You recoil at the itty bitty t-shirts in clothes shops for teenage girls that proudly state 'Future Muse' across the chest. Is that really what we want our daughters to aspire to? Because the idea of the female muse implies passivity, naivety, a silenced voice; objectification of the body and a willingness to be subsumed by that hoary old myth of the male genius (a myth enabled and sustained throughout the centuries by other males). Muse implies a female to be looked at and presumably slept with, a female who exists solely for male gratification. A female created by a male, tightly controlled. It's Pygmalion, Pandora, Galatea, an enduring myth that sits oddly and a little creepily with where the world is now in terms of gender relations. Who really considers the muse aspirational anymore? To you, the term exists somewhere alongside groupie and grid girl in terms of jobs for the ladies. A doormat.

~

You start planning a first novel, drawing on lived experience as first novels so often are. You write late into your desert nights of a passionate meeting, a storm and a creek bed, of being married under the elements. Yet you can't devise a way of how W's love would ever end, can't imagine a conclusion to that story.

~

The story of Camille Claudel is almost unbearable to read in terms of the thwarted female artist. Women who write feel too much – as do any women, perhaps, who choose the creative life. Claudel's works are charged with emotion. Passionate, honest, brave, ugly, sexy, radical in style and intensely alive. Her sculpture of Clotho – an elderly woman who spins the thread of human life, deciding when people are born and when they die – is painful in its brutal depiction of tortured, vulnerable old age.

When Auguste Rodin met Claudel he was immediately struck. She was in her late teens, he twenty-four years older. Rodin noted the vividness in the art as well as the vividness of the young creator behind it. He employed Claudel in his busy studio; one of her jobs was to model the hands and feet for his monumental *The Burghers of Calais* as well as his damned souls in *The Gates of Hell*. The two sculptors had a decade-long affair and during that time Rodin's work was influenced by Claudel. It became increasingly sensual as their relationship matured. His tender *The Kiss* was sculpted in this period.

Claudel's friend, art critic Octave Mirbeau, described her as 'a revolt against nature: a woman genius'. There are so many ironies to that statement because during that time, and for generations afterwards, a female genius was considered impossible, contradictory, a lie of nature. It is still considered an anomaly. Because, of course, it is white men who've always decided who geniuses are, and they're usually in their own image. Never female, never a person of colour, never Other.

~

With Claudel, history records that she had periods of mental fragility, but creativity was a tonic that kept her clear-headed and strong. She was saved by her art and when it was taken away from her she succumbed. 'You stole it all! My youth, my work! Everything!' Claudel wrote despairingly to Rodin in 1905. He didn't give her the one thing often needed to richly create as a woman – an inner peace.

Their sexual relationship foundered partly because he refused to leave his long-term, on-again off-again mistress, a seamstress, for Claudel. He gave her no clear space in her head and she became increasingly paranoid. She aborted his child and struggled to get commissions or make any money after she left his orbit. Claudel's work was deemed too erotic and dangerous for a woman and she destroyed much of it. Suddenly she was dependent on her ex-lover to survive financially; she sometimes still collaborated with him but then had to witness him becoming a celebrated giant of French sculpture. This fuelled her. She retreated to her studio to create works that might establish her own reputation but was ultimately unsuccessful. Despite the skill and fearlessness of her work, the establishment would not let her in.

The periods when Claudel was secluded and producing art coincided with times of calmness, firmness. The studio was healing. She suffered from mental decline when she was denied the space to create. Eventually she broke down and died in a mental asylum, living there for the last thirty years of her life and producing nothing. Doctors had recommended that she leave the institution five years after being incarcerated but it was up to her family to call it — and they treated her brutally. Claudel's mother and brother didn't want to assume any responsibility for her so they decided she should remain in the asylum. When she died her artistic legacy was all but forgotten. She was buried in an anonymous public grave.

Claudel's mother didn't approve of her talent. It was 'unladylike'. She wanted her daughter married with children. Claudel's father, on the other hand, was supportive of her choices. He approved of her vocation and helped her financially yet she wasn't informed when he died in 1913, and eight days later was admitted to a psychiatric hospital at the request of her brother, Paul.

Men devour us.

15

What you are gleaning, months into this relationship, is that you may have to rely on your own strength, alone, because the men in your life aren't quite strong enough to lean on despite conditioning to the contrary. Not even your father, who tries to persuade you to sink the profit from selling the Darwin house you'd purchased cheaply when you worked there, before Alice Springs, into his new business venture – which goes bust several years later. You can't understand that your father's financial whims seem more important to him than the sense of self-worth having your own money may give you.

You refuse him, even though it feels disrespectful, and instead invest the money in a flat in Kings Cross. You realise you will have to support yourself carefully, frugally and alone – because the men around you seem relatively weak money-wise and you don't understand why the world doesn't generally see that and talk about it. You don't understand why it feels like blasphemy to feel this, to articulate it. It feels like a revelation of growing up; that women are the stoic, constant, reliable ones. It's like you've been fed a vast lie.

~

Once again, no word from W for several days. Once again, he could run you off the rails. You hate the way his silence crashes into your calm, shifting your focus from writing. Again and again you become a hostage to his disrupting whims, his silence. But this is when the pen is picked up. When the sure path to the oblivion of love is disrupted. Is it wrong to say you're fuelled by anger? Why do you feel guilty even writing that?

~

You feel more intelligent than most men around you; watching, in wonder, that they get away with so much. Feel violently dissociated from your times, your history. Feel . . . knowing. Perhaps all women do. 'That is why Napoleon and Mussolini both insist so emphatically upon the inferiority of women,' Virginia Woolf wrote in *A Room of One's Own*, 'for if they were not inferior, they would cease to enlarge . . . they say to themselves as they go into the room, I am the superior of half the people here, and it is thus that they speak with that self-confidence, that self-assurance, which have such profound consequences in public life and lead to such curious notes in the margin of the private mind.'

~

February, five months into the relationship. W says in an airport cafeteria that he wants to marry you. You respond yes. 'Because it's right,' you say instantly, as simple as that. You love him, this will work, it is destiny, your future is sorted at last. His cheek is soft against yours. He says he will tell his best friend who'll be 'stoked'. You will tell no one yet. 'I will have it to send me to sleep every night,' you assure him. A secret held tight, in the clench of your heart.

And so to the distracted life of the engaged woman. Yet by marrying this man writing will not be at the centre of your life, you feel this strongly but dismiss it in the joy of normality at last. Years later you will read Elena Ferrante, who writes that a man marries to have a faithful servant and it is the reason all men get married. Yet you cannot see this at all with W.

~

Meanwhile, the bright gleam of the dream. There are a lot of obstacles to overcome before you will have the confidence to ever declare yourself a writer. You have had no one around you to lead the way. And you imagine that if you did eventually step across the threshold into the dream, well, who would celebrate it? You didn't have rows of bookshelves in your house growing up. The few tomes your parents owned were *Linda Goodman's Sun Signs* and the *World Book Encyclopedia* and a brace of red *Australian*

*Encyclopedia*s which your mother eventually threw out because she couldn't give them away.

Virginia Woolf wrote in *A Room of One's Own*, 'The world did not say to her as it said to them, Write if you choose; it makes no difference to me. The world said with a guffaw, Write? What's the good of your writing?'

You knew enough even then to keep your burning ambition very quiet.

With W, your drive felt like a dirty word. He made you feel like your intense focus on work and getting ahead meant you weren't quite living your life correctly.

~

When W doesn't call there's an agitation that comes from being gaslighted. There's no silence in your mind, no peace. The waiting inside you, for the gift of his attention, is like a dog with its head on its paws. When he's with you, there is no silence. He's a talker, swamping your thoughts with his opinion on books, music, art; veering your taste; so when he doesn't engage the silence feels deafening.

The phone rings. You jump. Cannot answer it. Do. Finally. It's yet another girlfriend asking if he's called. You're a hostage to his forgetting now. Everyone knows it. Then he calls, finally, and your world is made right in an instant. And you'd be happy to never write again if you had this forever; your own private sanctity, with him. Preston Sturges wrote that great men are the only things that diminish as you get closer to them yet W doesn't diminish because you never really know him.

~

The ultimate freedom is to act how you've wished to act your entire life, to be free of what others think. Does your partner allow you to? To be free to be who you really want to be. What do young girls give up on their way to womanhood? It seems increasingly to you that it's a journey into silence, uncertainty, meekness and that dishonest little word, niceness. Yet all this seems like a betrayal of that strong, sparky, stubborn and vividly honest child of eight or nine, the blazing girl who knew her mind and was in the ascendant. But then puberty hits and something happens through fraught, spiky, fragile adolescence.

The young female adult loses her sure grip. Her confidence. Becomes subservient to the God of Looks. How she herself looks, and how others look at her. Her mind is not valued, nor her voice, no matter how loudly it tries to speak her truth. The world just wants a pretty face and quietness and subservience; a willingness to do the bidding of men. A willingness to be trained to do the bidding of men. It's a troubling and perplexing journey from one world into the other, a journey into inauthenticity for many. The young woman is expected to be one thing while perhaps screaming inside to be something else entirely. There's a loss of voice, sometimes a loss of mind, at this crossing over into expected silence. The journey into uncertainty feels highly unnatural and destructive for some, a journey where you're taught to doubt yourself. It can be a path into victimisation and a grievous loss of identity. Edith Wharton wrote in *The Age of Innocence* of a 'curtain of niceness' that falls over young women as they pass from girlhood into adulthood, and it's an observation that's still applicable to this day.

~

Early March. You haven't heard from W, again, for a week. You are feeling savage. Fuck this abstinence; you're wanting, wildly. Crawling on your hands and knees and stuffing your face with biscuits and ice-cream and family-sized blocks of chocolate. Sick of the strict no-sugar regime, the endless swimming, the dribble-of-food starvation existence, all for him. To get the body of the girls he likes. Those inner-city girls with their sallow stance and A-cups, the groupies of the bands you've never heard of but pretend you have. So, just for tonight you are doing this. Forgetting, for an instance, the power of slim, and then floating through the next day with the strange, heady, exhilaration of a well-fed body. Because you have reclaimed yourself.

~

Your ABC boss is suddenly sending you to Darwin for two weeks to fill in for someone taking holiday leave. Exactly when W is due. You ring him, break it to him. It's only later that it hits. You want to sob, and sob, and sob. He rings, he wants to, also. Your work life is crashing into Us, and how you hate that.

~

Darwin has a wetness you can almost rub between your fingers and the grandeur of a ballroom in its cloud-crowded sunset skies. You buy a ring for W in one of the few antique shops left. A green stone for his eyes that looks black in the night light. You slip it on, again and again, and think of his long pianist's fingers seamed through yours. This will be your wedding ring to him, perhaps. Marriage is the crown of life – for a man – the conventional pinnacle of existence. But for a woman? It's a dissolving, surely. And that's the lie that's imprisoning you. Falling in love with a writer feels like the pinnacle of life; you couldn't aspire to anything greater. Because it's a match, a perfect one, surely; a meeting of minds that will initiate a great wellspring of creativity. Surely. Yet alongside it, softly, is a nagging sense of dissolving. A lie that is tightening around you. Perhaps.

~

A staff meeting. P, the boss, has flown in from Sydney for it. He's in his stride, addressing all staff, when he catches sight of you at the back of the room. He stops, in the middle of his speech. The stately bow of the head, the blush.

You had met at a dinner for the Darwin staff a few years previously, when you worked in that city. You both fell into impassioned talking and it was a conversation that monopolised the night. You could tell P was keen back then. Older men gave off a smell, of interest, that you would sometimes detect; it was as if their bodies couldn't quite help it. You did nothing with the knowledge, P wasn't your type. But you enjoyed his mind, what he had to say, the muscular vigour of his thinking. You parted as friends.

'How are you?' Later, after the meeting, to you alone. Unbearably intimate amid the crowd of colleagues. P wasn't expecting you here, in Darwin, you're usually in Alice. You blush, and his twinned blush, tells everyone everything. Yet not.

~

Will you regret this marriage? You don't think so. You don't need a towering alpha male like this big city boss before you, you can be strong and powerful by yourself. Not defined through someone else. Yet can W give you the freedom to be you, to worry at the dream? It all tugs.

You imagine a life of slog to pay the household bills on time, to hold everything together, while W writes in his splendid attic isolation. You shut the niggles out. This *will* work. Yet your own writerly chip of ice is giving you pause as this manager almost twice your age blushes before you; a friend from pre-W days who you've never slept with. But you know he's always wanted to, given the chance. And meanwhile the chip of ice whispers about a lifetime of slog while the man you love writes, which is your own bright gleam of dream.

But then P. A man who's had his driver fill the petrol in his car for so long that he's forgotten how to do it himself.

16

Photographer and painter Dora Maar tried to make her mark professionally while entangled in a relationship with a dominating male artist, in this case, Pablo Picasso. She found herself failing at both vocation and relationship. Maar had a successful photography and painting career before she met the Spaniard, but Picasso leaked his sneering opinions about the dubious 'art' of photography into the relationship, and her confidence faltered. Because unfortunately for Maar, photography was her principal art form, and one she excelled at.

Maar was twenty-eight when she met the 54-year-old Picasso. They were introduced by a surrealist friend, and their relationship took off after an encounter in a Parisian café in the mid-1930s. Maar transfixed Picasso by stabbing the table with a penknife that was shifted with lightning speed between her splayed fingers; sometimes she nicked them and drew blood. Picasso was smitten by the singular woman in front of him and asked for her glove, which was stained with her blood, as a keepsake. In a first for Picasso's lovers, she was a fellow artist who also spoke his mother tongue, Spanish.

Maar was at the height of her career when they met; Picasso was emerging from what he described as 'the worst time of my life'. He hadn't sculpted or painted for months. Their relationship had a huge effect on both their careers; Picasso's in the glorious ascendant, Maar's a descent into stagnation. She documented in photographs the creation of Picasso's *Guernica*, all the while stoking his political awareness and teaching him her artistic techniques such as the cliché-verre method, a complex practice that combines photography and printmaking.

Maar is most well known today as the jagged, broken muse for Picasso's *The Weeping Woman*. Yet during the time of its creation she'd gained a reputation as an accomplished artist in her own right, participating in the surrealists' prestigious group exhibitions. Her biographer Mary Ann Caws states that at one show Maar's *Portrait of Ubu* became an icon of surrealism. Her works examine ideas of the unconscious and sleep as well as female eroticism. If only she'd continued along that audacious, unsettling path – but her persuasive new lover belittled her chosen art form, and she was swayed.

Their affair lasted a decade. For Maar, it was a tragic period when her work's independence and singularity slipped away. She dropped her chosen field of artistic photography. Picasso didn't force her to, but she felt his disdain for so-called artists pursuing photography as an art form. He believed in the human touch as opposed to the mechanical and he associated the latter with photography. Sneering can be an incredibly destructive force, snuffing out the creative drive, especially with women who haven't been raised with the expectation that creativity is an acceptable path for them. Maar wanted to nudge closer to Picasso so her desire for his approval made her treat photography as a business option and painting – her lesser accomplishment – as her true vocation.

Seven years after the affair began the 61-year-old Picasso met Françoise Gilot, a 21-year-old artist. His new relationship bloomed as his one with Maar faded. In 1946 Picasso and Gilot visited Maar's studio together. As told by Gilot, Picasso forced Maar into declaring out loud to Gilot that her relationship with him was completely over. It was a humiliating set-up. With echoes of Claudel's experience with Rodin, Maar suffered a nervous breakdown at the end of her affair with Picasso. She was treated with electro-shock therapy and through therapy sought spiritual solace, eventually settling on Catholicism. This sustained her for the rest of her life.

Brigitte Benkemoun wrote in *Je Suis le Carnet de Dora Maar*, 'One could say that throughout Maar's life she wanted to be an artist rather than a muse.'

Much of her work was only discovered after her death. Her late works are not nearly as significant to the artistic canon as her surrealist photomontages were, pre Picasso. Was her brilliant career cut short by Picasso? Was she a victim of his psychological abuse, which chipped away at her confidence? Did she compromise by diminishing her great talent to please the man she loved? Art historian John Richardson said that Maar sacrificed her gifts on the altar of her art god. Her idol. It's highly likely she would have achieved a lot more without Picasso and what a tragedy that is. Maar's story of creativity thwarted demonstrates that it's all about confidence. How easily the sneering can get to women, especially if we're not meant to be good at a particular creative vocation in the first place. Because men have always told us so. Have elevated their own kind, have declared them the geniuses, have refused to consider the Other. It has not left women with very much space to nudge into the equation.

~

Why did these intensely creative female artists have their breakdowns? Claudel and Maar – and Plath, too – were all daring, accomplished artists in their own right. Yet when they met a fellow artist he became the rock upon which their own life broke, and broke, and broke. Was it the impossibility of keeping their own world together, as an artist; of doing what they really wanted to do in the face of the distracting headwinds of male creativity? Was it the torture of trying to maintain your vocation while someone you admired chipped away at your confidence? Your focus. Grit. Energy.

~

The writer Colette broke free, gloriously, from her tormentor – her husband, Willy. She had married at twenty. He subsequently discovered her writing talent and locked her in her room to produce, forcing her to write four *Claudine* novels which he then published, appallingly, under his own name. Despite the books being wildly popular, Colette saw nothing of her earnings. After thirteen years of marriage she broke free and produced her best work, managing to escape into a strong, independent creative life.

'It is absurd to suppose that periods empty of love are blank pages in a woman's life,' Colette wrote in her story, 'Bella-Vista'. 'The truth is just the reverse.'

When she left her marriage Colette was free finally to do what she really wanted to in life. She declared that she wanted to collect the few personal belongings which she held to be invaluable, and there were just three items on her wishlist. Her cat, her resolve to travel and her solitude.

17

An Easter weekend in April of saying no, to everyone. It's a rarely acquired bliss, when you hide away within a long weekend of solitude and unfurling, thinking. It's the relief of recalibrating. You're back to story – pure, writerly narrative – after so long. Everyone has gone away, no one is expected in your home, you have no social plans, and so you stretch like a cat in the glorious emptiness.

The artist Tracey Emin said that she feels physically ill if she doesn't create. That's always been you. But Emin has the luxury of time to work as a single, childless woman, she has no distraction. You are gleaning during these years of growing up that womanhood is a state of giving, helping, nurturing constantly, an enslaving distraction from what you really want to do. Unless you are happy to live with the label of selfishness, which you are not, yet.

~

In the luxurious expanse of a lone Easter weekend, you uncurl. The creative solitude gives you strength because you're doing what you really want to do. And you're starting to have an awareness of the personal price you'll pay as a sidekick to a dominating artist. What of those men who consider themselves the artist and their woman the facilitator of their art? You're gleaning a terrible truth during this time: that there cannot be two of you doing the same thing. You exist in this relationship to listen, placate, encourage; not to pursue with a single-minded conviction your own fragile vocation. You exist in the relationship to receive the wisdom of the dominant male, to nod, and smile, and revere. A man who has no idea of the curdling inside you; the immense watchfulness in silence; the enormity of your voluptuous secret. Oh, he knows you're 'dabbling' in writing around a regular job, but there is no real curiosity; your vocation isn't centred in this relationship. Unlike his. And as a writer, doubt is your invisible frenemy, always tagging along, goading you into giving up. You work secretly because you are afraid of failure.

~

According to Sartre, man's essential freedom is the capacity to say no. W is robbing you of the ability to say no yet you barely realise what is being taken from you. Femininity feels like a mass drug of indoctrination, turning you into someone else entirely, someone alien to who you really are. But like all good girls you're obediently drinking the Kool-Aid despite femininity feeling, somehow, like a con. Because it's not who you are. You're altogether something darker and stronger. Rage-filled. Honest.

~

At work you see P, the high-level boss once again visiting from interstate. Who always seems interested, who always has sexual tension with you, who has never so much as kissed you. You tell him of your engagement and he responds quietly, after a pause, that he's been infatuated with you for a very long time. You tell him you will always love him, despite the fact you've never had a relationship. You love him as a friend. He says he's so happy for you, that love is such an elusive thing and he recognised it in you straightaway. He says wistfully that your eyes are the eyes of a woman in love. You long for W as he speaks.

~

The day after this conversation you wake from a sleepless night and feel as if you've been through a spinner and have come out the other side grown up, a woman at last. Shedding skins. Extending a hand calmly, strongly, to destiny. P had said how cautious you'd been in the past, relationship-wise. 'Fortressed.' He tells you he never wanted to push it and, to his credit, he didn't. And so W stepped into the vacancy. Because desire is picky and contrary and rarely rational.

You cannot tell P that your reluctance to do anything with him is because you were never sexually attracted to him. But W, how you seized it. Knew right from the start and you're wet at the thought of him, still. It's always been this way, the knowing with any man, instantly, yes or no. And if it's a no it's very hard to persuade you otherwise. You feel deeply private, to the core. You will never let them know any of this. You watch, learn, gather, and write it all down.

~

W's engagement gift is a red dress from a cool Sydney shop. For Sydney. That world, his world. 'A dress my daughters will fight over one day,' he says with a knowing grin. The dress is long and spindly and hugs the body, it would turn you into something you are not. It isn't you in any way except for the colour. You don't do bare, don't do slink or vamp. When W gives you this red dress that you will never, ever wear you feel . . . not-seen.

~

'I am normal,' you write in your journal, 'but is this it? Is this what I've wanted, craved, for so long? I am not normal perhaps.' Doubt is your frenemy because you've been made to feel all your life that your maverick thoughts are not normal. Not normal because you don't want a conventional life. Not normal because you feel more intelligent than the men around you. Not normal that you don't enjoy sex. Not normal that you've never had an orgasm. Not normal that you don't want the cacklings of a narrow and reducing female group around you, nibbling away at you and dragging you into normality. Like them. So that their choices aren't challenged, so that disquiet never enters their world.

Tracey Emin wrote in *Strangeland* that a desire to be more normal is what pushes her. 'But as someone said the other day, "Trace, you're going to have to face facts. You and normal parted a long, long time ago."'

~

'You have never been curious about me; you never wanted to explore my soul,' Katherine Mansfield declared in a short story. You feel like you've lost the stillness at your core in the thick of this engagement with its red dress you'll never wear, a stillness you've always been able to retreat to. To be yourself in, unfurl creatively in, to write. W has robbed you of it. He disturbs your inner peace.

Suddenly, dangerously, you're at a crossroads. You want to toss your job away and just plunge into writing and art school and him, the dream of the other, artistic life. You want to make your writing somehow work alongside his. But could you ever actually do it? You can't quite articulate the dream because you're the only regular earner in this equation and quitting the ABC feels like a foolishly impetuous move. Yet you feel burdened by the slog, a radio reporter drowning in the stress of deadlines and gruelling shiftwork. The uneven start times are eating into your serenity and sleep, disrupting your period, and you're chafing at the bit. 'Risk girl, risk,' you write in your journal. Feeling poised, but for what?

18

In your neck of the woods, the outback pioneer known as Old Molly Clark is a legend. She lives in splendid solitude at Old Andado Station, deep in the desert. You interview her for a radio feature and drive along disappearing roads for hours to get to her, a lunar landscape of sand dunes and mysterious rain spots from the vast bowl of a blue sky above. Her rough outback shack is made of corrugated iron and eucalyptus posts and was transported on the back of camels in the 1920s from Oodnadatta, over three hundred kilometres away.

She is singularly her own woman. Her own self. It is electrifying. She has lived alone by a tall windmill for decades, with her trusty red LandCruiser to get her anywhere. She only has Vegemite for the scones she's cooked; neither of us could care less. She speaks of all the fancy geologists and scientists she comes across, who she declares have little experience compared to her years of knowing the land. 'If you could turn the bag inside out, I wonder what you would find.' Her fierceness works its way into you and spines you up. 'Dangerously, I feel the pull of it all. Want that away, that solitude, that madness,' you write in your journal that night. An away to write and be who you really are, uncompromisingly, like Molly.

~

Your best friend listens on the phone from Sydney to your chatter about the engagement and the blush from P in a work crowd and all the news of all the men, all the choices. 'You're in your prime, Nik. Just enjoy it,' she urges. Years later you recognise that the boss, P, would have given you financial security and freedom to write, as a man in an established career with his solid life. But you couldn't see it as a young woman in love with the idea of love. Desire got in the way and you were willing to risk everything for it.

~

W is with you in Alice for three weeks, then gone. It's a time of settling strongly into a rightness, a relationship, a couple. The rabbit sex dies down into something solider, firmer, older. The sweetness of skin to skin every night, the papery softness of his pale, non-sporty, inner-city skin. The night he leaves there is a rush to words. Feverish writing in your journal. It makes you feel . . . righted.

~

A video night with girlfriends. *Out of Africa*. A niggle of disquiet as you sit on the sofa with all these strong, young women of Alice. Adventurers, all from somewhere else, and established in their various careers with superannuation and mortgages; be it in journalism or medicine, science or art or linguistics. Strong, inspiring, independent women, every one of them.

Out of Africa is the writer Karen Blixen's story; a strong, financially independent woman with a handsome, feckless man. As you sit on the sofa among peers there's a niggle of maybe, one day, having to carry W. This generation of mates are the steady salary-earners, strong with money and cars and property, while the men on the peripheries of their lives whittle and wander, dabble and dream, sowing the seeds of a brilliance that's never quite seen. Yet. You wonder how the story will change as they age. This feels like a pioneering generation of solid, sensible, smart women, and their elusive men.

~

Meanwhile, a wedding scenario is firming. It will be next April. An autumn marriage. In your old school chapel, a heritage-listed jewel of white marble and woodwork transported from an old, disbanded convent in France. W's friend, a designer, will create your wedding dress. You'll move to Sydney over the summer. For him. You have six months to organise a retreat from the fierce little town that has given you so much; you want your ashes scattered here one day, that's how much it's wormed its way into your heart. Yet you will leave it all gladly for W despite declaring several years previously that you never wanted to live in a metropolis again.

~

June. A flying visit to Sydney. You sit in an inner-city café like a blind person, all senses reeling with the traffic roar and the snivel of a man sitting behind you and the radio jabber. You are drowning under the city assault, not knowing if you can do this again, if you can think in the midst of all this noise.

~

W and you break it to your mother together that you're engaged. It is fine, she's happy. The relief. But. The next day she rings you with a tone in her voice after a night of reflection. She wants to know if you're absolutely sure. If you'll be able to cope. With W. You tell her yes, everything's fine. Tell her that W has tickets to the opening night of the Sydney Film Festival, to distract and buoy her, yet it's not responded to generously and joyously but with a sing-song, 'What are you wearing? We dress smartly in Sydney you know. You don't want to look like an Alice Springs waif.'

You cannot speak, with rage. Do not think your mother will ever forgive you for not seizing the P chance; everything he represented. Stability and wealth, comfort and prestige. An easy life for a woman, to her. W is not good enough.

Just a writer. A scruffy poet in a garret. Destined to be penniless, with hardship and scrabbling and insecurity dogging his life. What is love to her? Transaction, security, a canny choice. And she's the only person in your life with the capacity to crawl under your skin and curdle there.

~

A weekend of telling the wider families begins with you, wrongly, asking W not to wear his lumberjacket at the crucial first meeting with your father (the jacket is inner-Sydney cool and ironic, but for you it's just too suburban, too close to the working-class Wollongong you grew up in. Dad won't get it. He'll think you're punching down.) W's flinch in response. You have hurt him for the first time. You both pause and sit on a bench at the train station, and miss the train. He says the day has started wrong. Asks what's wrong – 'Tell me, come on, what?' So you unburden. About the fear of carrying you both, of having a baby and not having enough money to live on or for the wedding. Of never being equal because you'll always have the steady job, exhaustingly, while he's in the attic being the writing genius and you'll have no time or energy for it yourself. He takes a deep breath and says okay. So maybe you go off to your parents, and he will go to his, and you'll both put the wedding off. For now. And by the end of the year, well, let's see. Suddenly, churning in you, is the panic of losing it all. No, you think, no! You're crying, wrapped in his arms. 'I love you,' you say, 'I want this. I will do this.

We will.' He nods. Cries. You decide to ring your families immediately, before the train journey.

You start with his parents. His father picks up. W tells him of the engagement over the phone, you listen in. 'Well, as Clint Eastwood said, you've made my day,' his dad says. Your mother's mother is thrilled. She talks of her own wedding to her second husband at the quaint Wayside Chapel in Sydney's Kings Cross; says in a babble how she never liked sex which makes you both laugh. 'We do!' You ring your father and W is taken aback by his formal words in response, 'This is something that should be said face to face.' But there's laughter bubbling through his voice. 'I'll sleep well tonight.' You ring a beloved aunt and uncle. Jubilation all around. At twenty-five, it is time.

Yet there's a vague unease within you. Are you losing them, with this? Losing your father? The next day he shouts you both to lunch at the place he met his second wife, an expensive formal restaurant – he's doing this properly. He shouts the whole family with great pride. It's working, all working, and you're brimful of laughter and love and relief. Any doubt is wiped in the messy, chaotic, giggly joy.

'You be strong for me and I'll be strong for you,' W says at your airport farewell. Daring you, lifting you, breaking you. Almost, perhaps, threatening you.

~

Back in Alice it's been a week and not a phone call, a letter, a word. You can't be strong in this alone. 'Don't fuck with me,' you write in your journal, 'or I will run if you do, from it all, and be lone, maddened lone. And write.'

You're lonely in solitude, for the first time in your life, as the details of the wedding settle like cement around you. W is sapping your strength and probably doesn't even know it. That singular, fierce, focused woman you were developing into is being rubbed out. W is confusing you, agitating and veering you.

'I think money, if anything, will kill us,' you write in utter coldness and clarity. Because being the wage slave to his art will kill you. You write that he's too selfish to see your own need. You go on a bush trip to Kings Canyon in the Watarrka National Park with a girlfriend. 'Is it my imagination or is this marriage thing ever so slightly sapping confidence,' is scrawled in your journal. At Kings Canyon you let your friend take control. Not particularly wanting conversation with strangers, retreating, shyer. 'I've never been this.'

He writes in a letter, finally, that he feels like you help him to live. But does he help *you* live? Your role is prop, supporter, worshipper. 'Yet it persists,' you jot down that night, 'this slight niggle of a feeling now I am to be married that I am somehow less. Just a woman, like other women, the little wife. Just a body, a brood mare, and accompanying it all is this subtle loss of confidence. Insidious, as I lean on another, as I become dependent on another.'

~

W and you aren't alike as writers. You work differently, are motivated differently. You do it furtively, in the cracks of your life. He writes out of expectation that his life will always be this, will always be accepted; you on the other hand feel like an imposter, the not-quite-deserving, not-quite-good-enough.

In his biography of Ted Hughes, Jonathan Bate describes the moment Seamus Heaney met Hughes. 'It was the assuredness of the sense of poetic vocation that most struck Seamus Heaney when he first met Ted Hughes: "the certainty of the calling from a very early stage . . ."' What woman has that assuredness. Dares to have it. That audacious writerly confidence.

~

'What mainly worries me . . . is a strengthening suspicion that in my character there is an antipathy between "art" and "life",' Philip Larkin wrote to a friend about his first love, Ruth Bowman. He said that once he gave in to another person, such as Ruth, 'there is a slackening and dulling of the peculiar artistic fibres'.

With W, you're too ready to give in and are starting to glean this uncomfortable truth. Love to hate is such a little leap. Because writing shelters you. You feel exposed and raw and unbalanced without it, trapped in a high wind of uncertainty. With W, maintaining the inner world is so hard.

Too hard, at times, too many times.

19

July. Wolverine. Stuffing and cramming and ripping and tearing at food and drink all at once, milk and chocolate and biscuits and peanut butter and oysters and bread because your body is craving it after months and months of denial, ever since W came into your life, that first day of the inner-city café. You revel in frenzy on a Friday afternoon after a long week of work. After six months of starvation. It feels good, so good, you can feel your deprived body grabbing at the milk, the peanut butter, the chunky nutrients as it all goes down. It is gluttony, fuel, strength. Because he is fading you. Fading you away, fading you out. And this is a gulping back of some kind of life.

'Sitting here on a precious day off from a six-week run of early morning shifts and exhaustion and a head cram of work worry and I'm thinking, *Do I really, actually, want this life?*' Your journal gets the brunt. 'I stare at an application for a current affairs reporting job in the Big Smoke yet do I really want to burden myself with the madness again, when all I want, really, is freedom to write? I've got to give a novel a go. But no time. Oh to flee from all this. Courage. That's what it'll take. Don't have it.'

It gets to the point where you think an absence of love would almost be a relief.

~

When Camille Claudel was Rodin's lover she wasn't submissive. You could never label her a pushover. She point-blank refused to live with her lover while he still had his long-term, seamstress mistress. Claudel's affair with Rodin was a scandal and when news of it reached her family her mother was mortified and enraged. She forced her daughter to leave the family home. During this tumultuous time Claudel was working on minor details of Rodin's sculptures alongside his other students. His big commission during this period was *The Burghers of Calais*, while she was also creating and exhibiting her own work. Many questions were thrown at Claudel. Could her work ever be seen as truly original? Was it influenced by her teacher? Would it ever be accepted as standalone works of art?

These cruel aspersions haunted Claudel. She was fiercely independent and ambitious and her style was unique, yet the slurs over her association with Rodin were artistically and mentally crushing. It was a way of erasing her, silencing her presence. Her work was actually bolder, more connecting, more emotional. The sensuality in her sculptures was acceptable for a male practitioner but seen as unseemly in a female; the double standards shocking and destructive. Financially, Claudel still had to depend on Rodin for collaborations after their relationship ended as well as stomach the knowledge that he was often getting credit for her work.

The question this sorry tale poses for the female artist: is staying with a male artist – working in the same arena – healthy for them? Will it stunt them to exist in their shadow? It's a conundrum at the heart of the creative woman's quest for a working life entangled with a romantic one. Sylvia Plath was prescient when she wrote in her journal, despairingly, that she desired the things which would destroy her in the end.

~

Celia Paul was a teenage art college student, fresh from school, when she met the painter Lucian Freud in the seventies. He was a teacher at London's Slade School of Fine Art; fifty-five to her eighteen. She met him on one of her first days at the college. He was smoking a Gitane, she was smitten; a familiar trope. A relationship began almost immediately and lasted for nearly a decade. And like Claudel with Rodin, the Freud relationship led to Paul being dismissed as just another muse in her famous lover's extensive catalogue of lovers and sitters.

Yet like Claudel, Paul was successful in her own right. Decades after the affair had begun she published a memoir, *Self-Portrait*, reclaiming her story; she centred herself, finally, in the narrative in the face of decades of reductionist labelling as muse, sitter, lover. She explained on the book's publication, 'I was "Lucian Freud's muse". I felt I needed to do something about this. I thought the way to do that would be to make this story my own.'

Her writing details Freud's initially forceful approach, despite there being an almost forty-year age difference. He insisted Paul lie naked, with all the defencelessness that entails, when he painted her. He imposed an acute, almost bullying vulnerability upon her which brought her to tears. There was Freud's demanding, selfish character and his frequent betrayals with other women. Yet Paul's story is a growing journey into creative empowerment. In Freud's last painting of her she stands fully clothed with her foot on a tube of paint, while a naked male model sprawls on a chaise lounge next to her. Freud is capturing the change from passive muse to fully-fledged artist in her own right.

Freud had initially encouraged the young Paul to think of their relationship in similar terms as the one between Rodin and yet another younger artist, the Welsh painter Gwen John. Rodin was long past his relationship with Claudel when they met; he in his sixties and John in her thirties. John had initially modelled nude for him; it quickly developed into a relationship. She abandoned painting for a time, to give herself up to, as she described it, the experience of being in love.

Early in their tryst Freud had encouraged Paul to give up her art. She says she might have been attracted to the idea if she hadn't known of Lucian's history. Paul knew another of Freud's girlfriends, Suzy Boyt, had stopped painting and Paul suspected he had said something similar to her. With Lucien, she felt 'there was always this element of control.'

Paul reassessed her relationship with the benefit of hindsight. 'When I was at the Slade several of the students were having affairs with tutors. The fact that Lucian said to me subsequently that he only came to the Slade to pick up a girl didn't at the time seem shocking to me, or to anyone there. Whereas now to me it does seem shocking.'

Paul now feels that after all her years of painting she's finally earnt her space away from the lionised alpha males of English art. She objects to the phrase 'in her own right', she says, as in: 'Celia Paul is also a painter in her own right. I want there to be no question that I am a painter in my own right.'

So, Paul has reframed the narrative with her own voice. She is no longer seen as merely Freud's muse. And why shouldn't it be that women claim the artistic space for themselves? Rather than others – that is, men – deciding how that precious, hallowed space should be claimed, and by whom.

~

Does sex ruin focus for the female writer, for any woman of ambition; does biology always get in our way? We are programmed to procreate. What young woman has not felt that sense of willing erasure at some point? Who does not long to feel it at some point?

~

The sixties 'It girl', Jacquetta Eliot, was also one of Lucian Freud's conquests who spoke of his modus operandi. He demanded she stop taking contraception. Told her she was his and he wanted a child. He declared airily, of other girlfriends, that it was nothing to do with him that they were having his babies. His biographer, William Feaver, said that to sit for Freud was to serve – and more often than not in more than one capacity.

Eliot and Freud's relationship was tempestuous. She insisted he write to their son, Freddy, to explain to the little boy he'd actually been wanted. Yet when they broke up Freud asked for the letter back; that was the monstrousness of his personality. He painted some of his teenage daughters nude, considering it a way of getting to know them better, according to Feaver's biography, as well as a handy solution to the difficulty of finding sitters. His explanation: 'It's nice when you breed your own models.' He devoured women and they succumbed willingly. Often. But the pain he left in his wake.

Part of the shock of the equation is that it's expected artistically minded men will somehow be more liberal, empathetic and generous, more open to the female artist and her own creative spirit. But of course that's not always the case. The ego and fallibility of man so often gets in the way, and shock over a rampantly selfish, creative male is perhaps greater for being, quite possibly, unexpected.

~

Is there an ideal scenario that exists between a young female artist and an older male master of their craft? Janet Frame gave a clue in her relationship with the short story writer Frank Sargeson, who offered her the use of a hut in his backyard, just for writing. Sargeson was gay, so there was never the complication of sexual tension between them. Frame wrote in her autobiography, *An Angel at My Table*, that her life with him was a 'priestly' kind of life, celibate and dedicated to writing. Frame flourished. In fact, Sargeson's offer might well have saved her life. 'It was not until I had been writing regularly each day that I understood the importance to each of us of forming, holding, maintaining our inner world . . . and how its form and power were protected most by surrounding silence.'

Oh for the balm of a surrounding silence. Agitated, you write in the thick of the engagement, 'Run run run run. Get out of this life / Slave life / (weary, so weary, wanting)'. You know that domesticity will deny you so much and have no desire to be someone else's doormat. Yet it feels transgressive to say this. To want something else entirely. Giving over your freedom to fulfil a biological want feels like such a hard bargain. 'I watched with envious wonder the lives of those women who, finding their "men", fulfilled not only their own expectations but those of their family and friends and thus added a bloom of certainty to their being,' Janet Frame wrote. You're fascinated by that bloom of certainty. See it in others, in girlfriends from your convent school days mostly. You desire it yet fear it too. What is needed is a renovation of your serenity – but you don't know how.

20

A visit to Sydney. W is late home without explanation. In the waiting dark you ask yourself a question: would you marry him if he has slept with someone else? You will not. How quickly the spark of passion can be extinguished, how quickly it can sour. Sitting by W's attic window, staring out at the night-bright street, you feel like you're waiting for an excuse to dive into writing. 'I want to write,' Marguerite Duras wrote in *The Lover*. 'I've already told my mother: That's what I want to do – write. No answer the first time. Then she asks, Write what? I say, Books, novels . . . She's against it, it's not worthy, it's not real work, it's nonsense.'

~

Cynthia Heimel said women have to keep creating their lives as they go, otherwise, as they age, they become invisible. Is it time to create something fresh? Because you now feel you're imprisoning your life, trapping it in amber.

Yet it's everything you've dreamed of. The writer, the books, the garret are the wish but it's W's dream and you don't stand alongside him as an equal in it. Because you've stopped. There are no words. No creating. A vast nothing.

~

Back in Alice Springs, joy. The Sydney-based literary magazine *Southerly* accepts a short story you'd written a year or so previously, about Darwin, before W. Soaring relief. You can still do this. This story is like a child you can now give away and suddenly, with newfound confidence, you're powering with the writing, feeling again the tug of risk. You are powered by the affirmation of an acceptance – courtesy of a literary magazine and not a bloke.

'W hasn't rung for a week and there's a little part of me that wants him to abandon it all,' you write in your journal, 'to leave me free to run away to a little tin shack in Tennant Creek to be tragic with my computer and chocolate and a vast sparseness. To write, just that. Tossing in the job, flat, man, friends, family and run from it all. The excuse for the plunge.'

Janet Frame, in *The Envoy from Mirror City*, wrote, 'Dr Crawley was clear: his prescription for my ideal life was that I should live alone and write while resisting, if I wished this, the demands of others to join in.' Joan Didion said that to free ourselves from the expectations of others – to give us back to ourselves – there lies the great, singular power of self-respect.

~

You're dissolving in W's presence and now his absence. He's the love object who you fear you can never find happiness with, yet you're enslaved to him. Romantic love is beginning to feel like a con, a cop-out, a wipe-out.

You cannot escape the intensity of it all. The love has lost its innocence. And there's a new hardness in him as he muses over the phone about money and wages and survival, about how this can all possibly work. You reply that the money thing is humiliating, you'd like it to be more equal; you don't necessarily want to be the super woman in the relationship. Can women have it all by not doing it all? You don't want to be the slave working to the bone in a job you don't like to provide the steady income for you both. Don't want to be not writing yourself, you do not add.

Yet you crave the house of the newly married, so tender and precious and rare; you want to live under that spell of enchantment where everything feels new and fresh and warmed by love. You've been revelling in this relationship because it feels like everything your steely mother doesn't want for you and you've always wanted to kick away from her strongly. Yet, yet. Your mother reinvented herself after the great liberation of divorce. She had been the model suburban housewife for twenty years until she could bear it no more, and demanded an escape, and firmed from that point.

~

Another rare day off from a run of exhausting early morning shifts. You spend the day listening to the radio and writing in your journal and thinking, again, *Do I really want this?* You decide to do something about it. Fill out applications for Sydney current affairs and news jobs that begin in the early hours, burdening yourself with the stressful madness all over again. 'I'VE GOT TO GIVE THIS NOVEL A GO' you scrawl in capital letters in your journal. But soon you'll have a husband to support and a marriage binding you, soon there'll be no time for creativity. It will be squeezed into the margins of your working life. Yet you want the writing, viciously, the claws of it will not let you go.

~

W addles you with sex. The thought of him dips your stomach. He is the first man who puts his lips to your sex and what a revelation it is; it feels like an act of generosity. There's a selflessness to it that you've only ever practised yourself, on other men. Later a male colleague your age – who you can be more frank with than any of your lovers – tells you that he hates going down on girls. Why? you ask. Because every girl tastes different, he says, and it makes him gag. You think of how lucky you are, how precious it is what you have with W.

Yet as a thinking, observing woman you hate what men reduce you to when it comes to sex. Legs wide, begging for it, you cannot help it. It is your body asking, demanding and it feels like your fate to surrender to this humiliation, despite knowing coldly and rationally that it's stealing your strength and will. It's a pattern perpetuated forever by women, the diminishing, because we beg for it. You dream of leaving W behind yet you're in thrall to him. You bow down before him, you submit willingly, again and again, and perceive nothing odd about this. Nothing odd in the erasure.

21

Late September, a week before W is to arrive in Alice. You live in slovenliness in a clothes-draped room with smeared white sheets from sleep upon sleep and dusty hair balls on the floor. Your eating routine now consists of an engorgement of food then starvation in an endless pattern. But the rigour has been given up in this final week, with the strain of the waiting, you're breaking down just before it begins all over again. 'I know Orpheus, I know,' you scribble in the journal. Falling, failing.

Poison mood. 'Fuck, man, is this going to work,' you write. Because W has put the visit off for a week. He has deadlines, as do you, yet you both deal with them differently; he stretches them out whereas you're always punctual and paced; the girly swot. He accuses you of being 'tight' and makes the way you always hit your deadline sound like a personality failing. 'I'm splintering with the strain of it all,' you rage in your journal. 'Cannot go on with this. I'm just like a big story of his where he keeps on saying, "I'll do it next week, it'll be finished on Tuesday/Sunday/next month." Fuck it, man. I've never known anyone to run so much from deadlines. Is this worth it? Don't drag me down.' You think of Patrick White's description of Australian men and the strong women beside them, those weak, emasculated men in their shadow; you think of the way W sometimes gets nervous when he talks to you and hate it.

~

A transgressive thought. That you don't like this, actually, don't want this, actually, want to be someone else entirely. You are crouched, watching, seething; wanting difference yet feeling grievously wrong for doing so. Feel so . . . reduced.

~

W writes, finally, reminiscing about his last visit and how he turned his face to your chest and you encircled him in your arms and it was like a refuge for him, to rest from the world. And all the tightness is loosened. All the darkness of complication wiped. After a balming visit you write, 'W's body is becoming deeply familiar, there's a volume of experience behind it now as my arm rests across his chest and my hand cups his heart.' And a few days later, 'Aaaah, what I must remember is that this is good, what I have, so good. Be strong, have faith. You'll pull through.'

~

November. There's a date, finally, to return to the newsroom in Sydney, too soon; it's suddenly, swiftly, official.
The news editor – a gentle, thoughtful gay man – summons
you to the ABC's headquarters in Ultimo knowing this is
what you want. He also knows W. He'll make it work for
you both, a plan is cementing. You will live with W in
his garret room before the wedding, your own flat after
it. 'I feel a great sadness, relief, fear and anticipation,' you
write as you prepare to leave your wild frontier home, the
place that gives you solace and strength. It will be hard
to let go of the land that's wrapped itself around you and
grown you up. 'I'll be leaving part of me behind, and will
hopefully return one day to reclaim it because my spirit
lifts whenever I return to the centre. I yearn for it when
I'm away.' Is this love with W a rescue? Or this land?

~

In the flurry of your last Alice days you visit a friend
out bush, a ceramicist living on the fringes of a scrappy,
abandoned chicken farm. Her old silver bullet of a caravan
nestles under a spreading tree, her cooking bench is set
up in the dappled sun and her books and clothes and
shoeboxes of letters nestle cosily inside. She is alone,
gloriously. No phone, alarm clock, radio. She has left the
world behind. Her pottery is set up in an empty chicken
shed. Her vegetable patch is thriving. She shares a fridge

with others like her, scattered on the edges of the property. A forbidding 'KEEP OUT' sign is at the gate.

The hum of the quiet. The blanket of stars above. The solitude. The uncomplicated, richly creative life. The beautiful rigour and spareness of it all. If you weren't getting married you'd be tempted to fall into this world. 'I'm a writer first and a woman after,' Katherine Mansfield wrote, but right now you feel like the woman in you takes over too much.

～

The final few weeks in your tough little desert town. Revelling in the company of ABC colleagues, the journalists and presenters you've grown very fond of over the past few years. They've seamed themselves into your life like family and offer words of advice on long-term relationships, on marriage. 'Always listen as you go into this.' 'We never do it enough.' 'The first two years are the worst. Getting used to the different personalities.' 'It gets better from there.' 'Just hang in there.' They have a sense of ownership over this forthcoming wedding – they've all been there with you during the courtship and have seen W in the office many times. You'll miss them very much.

～

Your penultimate day in Alice. Lying under a tree on the outskirts of town. The grass smells heady and sweet and you want to plunge your face into it. Birds are in front of you, behind and above. You feel achingly sad to be leaving yet quietly confident for what is ahead. A new cycle. An unknown life. For W and you together, to make very good if you can. A bird suddenly settles, very still, into the ground. The air is hot, tremulous, utterly still, as if all the world is waiting. A bank of cobalt grey encroaches fiercely to the west. You lie on the hard ground drained of all energy; a turbulence in the faraway sky is leeching your strength away. Your thighs will not work to push the pedals on your bike as you panic into a sudden escape. But then you stop, must, for a photo to capture all of this. *This* is what is to be reclaimed. One day. When you're back.

A soft rumble in the distance, thunder or a road train, you can't tell. An approaching roar through the trees, a dying out, and again. Bellies of pink arc above as Major Mitchell's cockatoos swoop by in a sudden evacuation. The smell of eucalyptus is flint sharp in the air. Ghost gums are dramatic in coats of stark white against the eery light; it's their moment – look at me. You vow to remember all of this, all, in the fist of your heart.

22

December. You smell the salt on the breeze as you step from the plane, the whiff of it in the gap of the passenger chute. Shiny cars, all new-looking, sparkle in the Sydney sun. You don't get that kind of wealth in Alice. W is waiting and the shudder begins in your bowels and travels deep to your breast, almost hurting, at the sight of him. That night in his garret the pillows are infused with his smell and you breathe it in deep to quell your restlessness. Later, wrapped in darkness, you write, 'First night in Sydney, feeling stranded, in limbo, not on holiday anymore but nowhere to go home to. Can't go back to Alice. It's gone. My world, my beloved anchor.' It feels like you must grab at nature in this city return. To come from such a stunning land and find a fresh calm you have to track down something equally soldering. But can you, anywhere, here? In this rushing, too-noisy, light-saturated place.

~

Women's lives tip constantly into complexity with the way we constantly hold things together, help, prop up, organise. Men aren't called upon to multi-function in such a way. They have the arrow of focus to pull them more cleanly through life. A woman's focus is scattered by so many competing pressures. 'It is the only life I care about – to write, to go out occasionally and "lose myself" looking and hearing, and then to come back and write again,' Katherine Mansfield wrote. 'At any rate, that's the life I've chosen.' It's what you want, but don't quite know how to seize it amid shiftwork and wedding preparations and an impending Christmas with all the family presents to be bought. 'Risk! Risk anything!' Mansfield urges deep in the night. 'Care no more for the opinions of others, for those voices. Do the hardest thing on earth for you. Act for yourself. Face the truth.'

~

Your father allows the two of you to stay in a derelict wooden beach house he's bought in Newcastle which he'll soon knock down to build a dream home for his second family. There's nothing left in the dwelling now but a mattress on roughly painted white floorboards, a kettle and a shower that's a piece of iron piping jutting from a wall. W and you move in just before Christmas. He's beside you every morning as a lemon sun pushes its way into the simplicity, among the newspaper scatter and the book piles and the sheet-mussed bed. Have you ever been happier?

~

Christmas Day, your first at home after many seasons away. You've been dreading this kind of crammed family Christmas for years but it's good, it works, everyone's on their best behaviour. There are engagement presents and separate gifts for W, there's laughter and joshing – you, married, finally! – and it feels like a familial enfolding of you both, a binding with a myriad of lovely, tiny threads.

~

January. Changed plans. You'll move into your Kings Cross flat you've never lived in before, to set it up. W will follow in a few weeks and you'll start your living together before the wedding that's to take place in the cooler, mellow autumn. 'The first night in my Kings Cross flat,' you write. 'Tumultuous. Too alive, too awake, with all the sirens and footsteps and garbage trucks and shouting. And underlying it all is a strange, white-noise rumble of the city that never stops.' You're perched high above the fray but feel in it, eye-deep in wakefulness, ears alert. You can't shut anything off. 'Is this what I want? This life, from now on, this never-dark, never-quiet.' There was never any question about W moving to you in the desert, despite him living the freelancer's life. Of course you would move to his city, of course you would leave everything you loved for his world.

The third night. Tumult, again. Mosquito-addled dreams. There's a well of complexity within you that W will never understand. There's so much women are expected to do, to be; so many expectations upon us. Men feel like simplicity personified in comparison. They're fortunate to have that focus, it gives them space. To create. The serenity of space.

~

W moves in finally to the flat you have a mortgage on that was bought with the proceeds of your offloaded Darwin house. You wake together and cook bacon and eggs and W gets dressed for his first day ever where he actually 'goes to the office' – in his old garret. He has not given it up. You kiss him goodbye and bury your face in the softness of his neck and savour this moment in your new, wifely life. And you never wonder why W doesn't give up his old bedroom, despite perpetually lamenting he has no cash. It's as if he knows something you don't.

~

'First day of work. Sydney newsroom. 4 am start. Bushfires springing up and back in the thick of it and adrenalin pumping and suddenly Alice seems very far away and there's a glimpse of how people lose it.' You try concentrating solely on reporting work, no time now for any other kind. 'Deep into the rhythm of early shifts and the panic is clutching me,' you write that night. 'There's no other life but this when you're in it. Work sleep eat work sleep eat, the rhythm kills, a blanket on your brain.'

There's an ache for Alice. Ash flakes settle on the bathroom's white tiles even though you're forty kilometres from any fires. You go to the roof of your eight-storey apartment block and dirty brown bushfire haze is billowing to the right and left, and the startling sun, a fluorescent orange–red, is like an apocalyptic moon through ash cloud. Later the sky is black, in daylight. Ash black, death black.

~

A hair cut in a Kings Cross salon. The busty blonde in her tiny, scruffy space smiles knowingly. 'You're from the country, yeah?' 'Yes. Alice Springs.' 'I can tell.' 'How?' She smiles. 'There's something different about you.' You feel country naïve. Explain you're new in town, living in a nearby flat, that you have a job and you're with your fiancé. You can see her filling in the picture of this country-glow girl and wondering how long it will last. The marriage.

You want Alice. A simpler way. Because in the city you can't simplify your life and it'll only get worse. Can you really do early shifts all over again? They're violent in the disruption to your life and equilibrium, messing profoundly with circadian rhythms. Some women don't menstruate on them, others find it hard to fall pregnant.

~

The birds are still, late in the day, on the rooftop and apartment gables and high clotheslines; they wait as if knowing something you don't. A black feather – a crow's – appears on the white tiles of the bathroom floor. W says the black crow is his totem, it's what he was told in Arnhem Land long ago. You feel very far away from that world. Which nourished you. Time is being eaten up so quickly in the rush of the city and the extreme demands of shiftwork. But you cannot give up, cannot stop.

~

'W touches my unit, my own space, so lightly. I don't like it. I want him to give it a chance.' Soon after you write this there's a tight knot of anger and frustration when you cook dinner for him and he doesn't come, doesn't explain. You turn to your journal once again. 'Don't fuck with me, mate. Don't fuck with my life. You think I'm the chattel, the little wife? Fuck it, no. Get me free.'

Vomiting into the toilet bowl; it's like a violent reaction to the city itself. To the smog and head cram and shiftwork and bushfire smoke and ash, to the never-stop of it all. 'Oh for out,' is scrawled in your journal. Because the city swallows up time. You have space to think, to unfurl, out bush. You curl on your bed high up in the sky and dream of a silver caravan in the middle of nowhere, yearn for the rescue of it.

'Bastard dream on this early shift. It's all started again. The mind fuck. I'm in the hallway outside, summonsed by neighbours, the doors won't lock and we have to keep vigil. So, no sleep. Me saying to myself, "Sleep, get some sleep" but I can't then the alarm goes off at 3.20 am and I wake up traumatised that I've not slept an entire night. Yet I have. But I dreamed I hadn't, not a single wink. Bastard dream.'

~

February. An Indian restaurant around the corner from your flat, for dinner. It feels grown up to go out like this, rare and expensive. W has suggested it. And over the meal he tells you that he's having second thoughts, to maybe give the relationship a year, to just wait and see. That it's all been too fast, there's been no time to get to know each other properly.

You're blindsided, reeling. You tell him you will not be around in a year. He will lose you. Ask him why. 'Because of the money . . .' he stops. Ah, that old friend. Again, weighing so heavily upon him. You look at each other, suddenly wary. Realise that you don't know each other at all; in this moment he's a stranger to you. You had no idea he was thinking of this vast stopping, had not seen it coming.

Anemone, all senses flinched; you murmur a jumble of words about courage and risk and the fearlessness of not running away, that it's too easy to do all that. You want to shake him and shake him, shake the weakness out of him, all the procrastination and hesitancy and doubt. You tell him you have to be a team to make this work. Ask him where his sense of adventure is, all the while knowing you're losing him, he's already gone; your words are like water dribbling away into sand and there's nothing, nothing to hold them firm because he's decided this. By himself.

The future is closing over you as you sit there, seeing yet not seeing, in a pit of mortification and helplessness and embarrassment. This is failure and you sense you could go mad with it. In this Indian restaurant where your whole world – living arrangements, city, job, future – is falling apart around you and you cannot stop any of it. Fix it. You have lost control of your life, for the first time. You feel eviscerated by vulnerability.

Your palms press into your temples. Not sure you can go on. How can you go on? Face everyone? Anyone?

23

You look up, finally; look him in the eye in that Indian restaurant. And want to do something very reckless. W is the love of your life and you've been loudly proclaiming it, to everyone. Is there anything more painful than unrequited love? You feel the abyss yawning before you and want to step into it and be swallowed up.

～

'I do not feel suicidal, which is good,' you write later that night, after W has returned to his old share house.

You slip out of your apartment and wander the light-buzzy midnight streets, passing people still cramming restaurants and bars. The world feels brimmed with happy chatter, all around you, it's all you see. Couples kissing, holding hands, arms around shoulders, hugs. You can't go on. Want to buckle in the glare of the Kings Cross streets, sink to your knees and howl. You keep walking, blindly, somehow.

So this is it. Loss. Heartbreak. Where to begin, where to end. Your head is throbbing with the ache of it all, with trying to answer all the questions. You fear W's hesitancy, his motive. Is this some game to test the mettle? Has this grown bigger than either of you intended? And is this it? That's the big question now. The question you cannot face.

Tear-streaked, mind-battered, you walk those midnight streets. And all the while the enormous muscular love for W is strong and pushing, pulsing, under the cluttery rest; the sneak of his uncertainty and your lurching shock. It is a love for W that's Grand Canyon big, that you do not know what to do with now. Lamed, stumbling, you fumble open your front door, curl on the ground in the hallway and sob, and sob.

~

Your father rushes to see you the next day. 'Have you got that an-plexia or something? Get some food stuck into you.' He says if you somehow go through with the marriage after all this, it will bankrupt you emotionally and financially. 'You'll get six years down the track and say, "What have I done?" And you'll have nothing.' An indignation roars through all his words, the indignation of how dare W do this to his daughter.

Your father explains that it will be three years of grieving and then you will be clear of it and will not look back.

Three years, because he has experience. He has belonged to that exclusive club, heartbreak, from the time when he split from your mother. Three years? Quite possibly it will be a lifetime.

Your mother, on the phone, says, 'I just wish I was there to hold you.' Like she always knew how it would end.

~

'This has galloped away from me,' you write in your journal a week later. Your eyes are scratchy with tears and hurt and your head is still throbbing with the ache of trying to see it all, still; trying to glean W's perspective. 'It's like a block of wood has smashed across the side of my head.'

~

'He's a pro at this, Nikki. In one way or another he's done it before.' You jot the many conversations with your father in your journal. 'He can't live with you having the flat, the car, having more. He can't support you. And a marriage can't survive competition within it. He's been like this all his life and he won't change. He's trying to drag you down to his level. It's what wrecked the coalmining industry in the early eighties, they tried to drag the achievers down to their level and it ruined everything. He just wants someone like him, living in a tent in the outer suburbs. What life do you want? You make the choice. It's a different mindset. He's not a worker like us. He'll never give you support.'

Your father tells you that God's hand will be on your shoulder, guiding and supporting, and you just have to trust. Dad's wife, your stepmother, says society won't let a woman have more. Ever. Won't let her wear the pants. Earn more. Be more. She says a man's pride will always get in the way.

~

In those reeling weeks afterwards you abandon the core of who you really are, you forget yourself in the crazed hurt of it all. Become someone you don't recognise. Needy, obsessed, deeply vulnerable, self-hating. Is there a greater pain? You love this person but they don't want to be with you, and there is no way around it. But you can't accept it. Yet must.

'Don't you want to be with someone who really wants to be with you?' your mother asks, which gives you pause. Yes, of course. Yet you've convinced yourself you'll never find anything like this love again; no one will ever love you with such intensity. You've blown your chance forever at a big, romantic life.

Your grandmothers and aunt toss out blankets of comfort. 'Plenty more fish in the sea,' and 'You'll love again, but it will be better, stronger,' 'Put that red lipstick on, girl, and show him what he's missing out on!' 'Time is a great healer,' 'One day you'll find a love that's simpler, I promise,' 'Relationships can hurt less you know.' You can't see any of it. He was the one. There will be no one else. No one will love you like that, and you will never love like that again.

~

The wedding ceremony is booked for the chapel at your old convent school. The impending world of dress fittings and wedding invitations is all around you, still; you've been holding off cancelling everything in the hope of – what? A repairing, humiliatingly. Because the wedding preparations had made you feel like you belonged for the first time in your life among those females like your ex-classmates obediently settling down, falling into that pattern of the regular, successful female life. That you were normal after all; getting married had felt like success. And you were a perfectionist. This was to be the triumphant homecoming and you had been whooping at it all like a hat flung off into the sun. Normal, at last.

The words of Virginia Woolf in *A Room of One's Own* are only just beginning to be understood. 'I thought how unpleasant it is to be locked out; and I thought how it is worse, perhaps, to be locked in.' Because you saw only obscurely then that marriage could be an impediment to the factors that make life glorious for a woman – friendship, education, creativity, freedom.

~

A while later, suddenly feeling suicidal in the vast roller coaster of the breakup's ups and downs, the trauma of pain receding then rushing back, of fear and savage loneliness and a fresh feeling of drowning, again and again. You think of jumping from your high apartment window, or the roof terrace, of striding into the sky. You want W to be viciously haunted. By all of it. Forever.

'I was going to get married once,' you write in your journal. 'It ground to a halt just before the wedding. He was a man who was never quite comfortable with the worker and the money-earner in me, so I modified myself. Reduced myself. For him. I said to my mother in the rubble of afterwards that I'd never love as deeply or richly again and she smiled knowingly and said I would, and it would be deeper and richer and stronger, and I thought quietly at the time, yeah right, what does she know.'

~

Your grandmother organises a catchup with W's parents. He rings afterwards to say he's angry that you've brought his family into this; but it's okay, everything is still on track, he still wants to marry you.

Reeling. Confused.

Everything feels wrong now. Broken, dishonest, past tense.

There's no sense of love as a rescue anymore.

In another call W tells you that you're making a mountain out of a molehill, yet the sands now feel like they're constantly shifting, like there's nothing stable to grasp onto.

~

W returns to the flat one night to clear out his few possessions. You ask him if he still loves you.

'Yes,' he rasps, 'yes.'

How foolish you've been. You know in your heart that he was right on that night of the Indian restaurant: it would never have worked. Yet you can't quite detach. Can't let it go, just like that. But must.

'As much as I love you?'

He looks away.

At the end of the long night W says, 'I can't make a commitment to this wedding.' You're going in circles now, back at the beginning of the end.

'Well, it's over, then,' you say, calm and quiet. Because you are better than this. You have decided.

You are free.

~

You wonder if W will ever write a novel. His dream. You don't know. You think back to those people in your creative writing class at university who would turn out their paragraphs of exquisite prose but would never publish a book because they didn't have the grit, the drive, to follow it through. You sense something of this with W. That it will be years, perhaps decades of this ahead of him. Yet you think eventually he will do it – but you won't be along for the ride.

24

Being good never got you anywhere. Being meek and quiet and subservient keeps women quiet and in their place; a lesser, colder place. Even though you've been conditioned your whole life to believe that being good is how a successful women must exist. The curse of obedience has always snapped at your heels. The curse of female approval and its scourge, perfectionism.

It took you years to perceive the quest for perfection as a blight on womanhood. A leading girls' school in England has launched an exam that's impossible to get full marks in, to stop its students becoming obsessed with being 'Little Miss Perfect'. An online maths test contains questions that become progressively harder and when the girls reach the top of their ability they face problems they can't answer – which teaches them that it's okay to not get everything, always, absolutely correct. Perfection is an affliction that has to be unlearnt.

Your marriage, man, wedding and living circumstances felt like the image of perfection at the time, in terms of how you were perceived by the outside world. And you'd never experienced such a crushing failure as that moment when W walked away. It forced you to take a long hard look at everything. Your blindness, naivety, tightness, flaws. To reassess and learn – that you couldn't control everything.

~

You begin to see that W is right; he's doing you both a favour by walking away from this wedding.

'And I knew that in spite of all the roses and kisses and restaurant dinners a man showered on a woman before he married her, what he secretly wanted when the wedding service ended was for her to flatten out underneath his feet like Mrs. Willard's kitchen mat,' Sylvia Plath wrote in *The Bell Jar*.

~

You learn that taking risks and failing are as much learning experiences as a striving for perfection, if not more. What counts is what's learnt from the process, so that you don't get crushed when things don't go your way, because it so often doesn't in life. What woman wants a life held hostage by the fear of failure? Perfectionist tendencies are the enemies of open-mindedness, flexibility, relaxation – and that wonderfully loosening ability to laugh at yourself. All qualities that contribute to successful interactions with others and, crucially, happiness.

~

W crashes back into your life once again, leaves, you don't see him, you bump into each other awkwardly in the street, sleep together, it feels wrong, again you almost throw yourself off a high ledge. But eventually you summon the courage to ring your old school and cancel the chapel. And that's it. What feels like the end. In your heart the whole sorry episode is now past tense, even though it will take you years to fully recover from it.

~

Your teenage cousin, years younger, offers up wisdom from her perspective. 'I gave my boyfriend everything. I left school for him. Gave everything away. And I lost my self-esteem. I couldn't stand in a room and face people and I used to be so strong, about everything. And he's weak, the weakest person I know. W is pulling you down.' You know it to be true. You will never soar high with him even though, on his part, it's entirely unintentional. He's a kind and thoughtful man yet has no idea, and he's doing you a favour.

~

W tells you in the wreckage of the breaking up that all his other girlfriends have been unhappy in some way.

'Are you trying to make me unhappy too?' you ask him. 'Is that how relationships work for you?' He looks at you in bewilderment. He muses, 'I don't know.'

~

Some friends have the gentle glow of the just-married. One is having her second child. You want all that achingly, can't deny the animal urge, can't push away the fact that biology is taking over and prodding you to get a move on in this department. You think of some women's seemingly comfortable, easy, click-into-place lives that have never known parental divorce or poverty or trauma. So smooth, so effortless, or so it seems. And amid it all there's your aloneness; savage and dark and ugly. Everything still hurts and you hate it, that you cannot shed it. A falling. Again. The window, the rush, again. The step into the sky, one little step, is all it would take.

No. You cannot do it. To all of them. Your father, mother, grandparents, aunt, cousin, friends, colleagues. One night, before sleep, you put out a hand to a god if there is one. You've so rarely done this in life. You put out a hand and sleep, finally sleep. It will be okay. You will get through this. You are being pulled through it by the love that is around you, and it is enough.

~

The failure of this relationship leads to a loosening within you, a vast letting go. Because the traits of the perfectionist were straitjacketing your life and W had gleaned it. Wrangling short stories over sixty drafts, honing radio pieces until 4 am, refusing to appear in public without a full armoury of makeup on, positioning yourself carefully under a man during lovemaking as if there was a camera watching and, most tragic of all, being unable to just dwell in moments of happiness, to lie back in life and bask.

Ahead is a vast reckoning. A heft into simplicity. That's the goal now, guided by the voices of the women who've been carried with you on this journey. Colette and Janet and Sylvia and Doris, Virginia and Marguerite and Charmian and of course Katherine, who wrote in a letter to a friend, 'I am always conscious of this secret disruption in me.' As are you. And you're learning that rupture isn't so bad at all but good, cleansing, necessary. It will grow you up. Catapult you into the courage for a writing life.

'For it would seem – her case proved it – that we write, not with the fingers, but with the whole person,' Virginia Woolf declared. 'The nerve which controls the pen winds itself about every fibre of our being, threads the heart, pierces the liver.' Yes. You can do nothing else. Even if you fail at it you have discerned the vicious truth: you are obsessed, not by a man but by writing. Day-to-day reporting, at a desk in a newsroom, begins to feel like a sickness in the heart but it will take years to fully extricate yourself from it. Yet the seed has been planted and by W, this is his legacy. 'You put me in touch with my own soul,' Katherine Mansfield wrote once, and for W's actions you are grateful. The path is wide open to step into who you really want to be. Through all the darkness the silver bullet in the desert has been beckoning and it now feels like an exhilarating freedom to aim for. 'Very few people do this any more,' Sylvia Plath wrote in her journal, of being who you want to be. 'It's too risky. First of all, it's a hell of a responsibility to be yourself. It's much easier to be somebody else, or nobody at all.'

~

One night, during the ashy end of the breakup, W bursts into your flat at 4 am. He still has a key. He says it's gone too fast, what has happened, and this is not what you want, surely, is it? You reply calmly and rationally that you've moved on. 'You gave me the freedom and I'm taking it,' you say simply. 'I've discovered through this all the things that I really want to do with my life – and I'm going to do them.' He pauses. 'I've been very weak,' he says softly. Has he? You tell him, gravely, quietly, that you want to seize this now. Somehow. That you've found your freedom and feel like a fish who's slipped through the net. You don't tell him that you've lost respect for him and that this feels fatal in a relationship, and that you know from now on you'll lose respect for any person who tries to control or diminish you, even unintentionally. You'll back away quickly. From anyone who doesn't let you be how you really want to be. W isn't bad or vicious or monstrous, he's a good man. He just doesn't see you.

~

A new life opens out before you. You're unbound. You're shaking off the curtain of meekness, learning selfishness, practising loudness. A long journey is ahead and it feels like a gift, of experience. It will allow you to move on into a clear, clean, solitary space, to write. You feel richer and deeper and more receptive – and you now have empathy for others who've been in that barren, brutal club called heartbreak. Which no one wants to join.

~

A week before your wedding that isn't, you borrow your dad's caravan and moor it in a caravan park on the shores of Lake Macquarie, north of Sydney. 'Everything has stopped,' is scrawled in a looser hand in your journal. 'Suddenly I see the sky again. Breathe out. For what seems like the first time in over a year. This feels like a tonic. That crushed-in Sydney life – all window rush and stepping out from ledges and towering drops – is gone and now there is this. Stillness. To repair.'

25

It will take years to detach from the addictive, grimy, sweaty physicality of it all – the memory of W's lips is too vivid under your fingertips in photographs you can never quite throw out. Take years to be free of the urge to touch the black-and-white pictures of a dog with 'No Food' on its back, and of walking on an empty rail line in the desert, and of a bogged car in a creek bed. Years to be rid of the liquid stirring in your groin at the thought of him.

So often in life we love the things we're not meant to; the question, of course, is what we do about it. Then came those ending words – 'I can't do it' – at a restaurant, when your life imploded. 'It isn't you, it's me,' W of course said but instinctively you felt this must be your fault. You're a woman after all, with a lifetime of conditioning that it is your problem, always, that you are the one in the wrong. The journey of these years is a quest into how to 'un-lady' yourself. How to throw off all the conditioning from childhood onward that's been telling you to be quiet; to accept the dissolving of your true self. That erasure does immense mental damage to so many women. Decades later, you are still climbing free of it.

~

In the mess of the aftermath you see it clearly: W is 'the writer' and you've been subservient to that, to the consuming nature of his art. And it was slowly disappearing you. You wanted to write too, novels, yet there was never space for that in the relationship. You'll never succumb again. Never again subsume yourself to a man.

~

Faltering. Again. Your father wings you with unconditional love. Rings your ABC boss because you're too distraught to explain the deep trauma of the situation to anyone beyond family and closest friends. You're given immediate leave to recover, ten weeks, and bless that good manager. You had left Alice too soon and crave a return, a soldering. You jump back into your trusty ute with a shoebox of mixtapes (your own choices for the first time, not some bloke's), your swag and Z, an American girlfriend who's also gone through a recent breakup. The two of you drive halfway around Australia and stand in the middle of empty roads that are ringing with light and humming with silence, dressed in your blunnies and jodhpurs and bras and shout obscenities at the tall hurting blue, and repair.

~

Slowly, slowly you emerge blinking into the light. Into a fresh world. You are different in it. All your hesitancies – of being rattled, confidence-wise, under the thumb of a man – are gone. You've found the push to just do it. Write. The dream of the silver bullet in the desert tugs. You want W to be interviewing you one day, not you supplying the research for his writing glory, not you waiting for him to come home from some work gig while you've put the children to bed; too exhausted to ever write yourself. You have your swag and your stars and your notebooks and it feels like a vast recalibration. A re-set. Into firmness.

~

You have one wish now – to live a life more fully, and observantly, with more stillness in it. You are ready. Finally. You will love differently now. Seek different, nourishing things. You have learnt.

~

In 1968 Ted Hughes was in a relationship with the aspiring poet Assia Wevill. Fractiously. She wanted to repair what they had and possibly move back in together; she asked him whether he still felt 'the animal thing between us'. Or, she wondered, perhaps he just wanted her back to look after his two children with Sylvia Plath, as well as their own daughter, Shura. Ted made a suggestion. If they were going to live together again they should both consider writing down some new rules. He proposed that each of them draw up a wishlist of how the relationship could work.

Half-jokingly, Hughes drafted his 'Draft Constitution: for suggestions and corrections'. He described his own list as a 'row of horrors'. The kids were 'to be played with'. Their clothes mended. Bedtimes supervised and two or three hours a week had to be set aside for German lessons. There would be no cooking that Ted would have to do, 'except! In emergencies.' At least one meal a week had to be something new and Assia must provide basic cooking lessons for his daughter, Frieda, who was almost eight. A daily log must be kept of expenses. There must be an acceptance of all Hughes's friends. No dressing gowns in the morning. No sleep during the day, unless it was an emergency.

Assia's rage can only be imagined. She had had a successful career in advertising and wanted to now establish herself as a poet, yet Ted wanted her to be something else entirely. Assia informed him to 'forget the detail' and never returned to the home. Then killed Shura and herself the next year, as a final fuck you. Sylvia Plath had written in her journal, two years into her own relationship with Ted, 'we are amazingly compatible, but I must be myself – make myself and not let myself be made by him'. A decade before Ted wrote his domestic wishlist for Assia, Sylvia had written that she was tiring of Ted's liking for giving 'orders'.

'Beware the controlling man,' your mother told you once, in warning, early on. And you've carried those words with you all your life, and paid heed, and never allowed yourself to fall into their trap.

~

With W it had been a classic coup de foudre. Literally a sudden shock, a thunderbolt of love. You hadn't loved a little, quietly and calmly, you were wild with love. The psychological term, 'limerence', means an obsessive love, like a drug; you are addicted to the other person. And so you were. Lost. Until W you'd wanted to shake off tiny worlds; yet with him, increasingly towards the end, all your focus was turned inward to the bedroom and hearth, to cooking his dinner and preparing his lunch for a day in his garret. And it felt like only one thing could save you. Writing. But you had no time for it.

~

When Sylvia split from Ted she declared that living apart from him was wonderful – because she was no longer in his shadow and it was heaven to be liked for herself alone, and knowing what she truly wanted. She wrote her best work when out from under him, fuelled by anger. Your writing is often motivated by anger. You write best under its spell. Cleanly. Anger propels you. Why are men often allowed to own the emotion, but women aren't? You will make a novel happen. Finally. This will be the start of it. It is your pledge to yourself. You will make it happen by shedding burdens.

~

Within the vast new emptiness you uncurl, and write. A car is a woman's shed and yours becomes your writer's workroom. You and Z re-learn happiness, among women, on this repairing road trip halfway around Australia; the two of you are as happy as goats in gardens with sketchpads and notebooks. You have always loved going somewhere you've never been and your soul unfurls over these long, loose weeks, gunning along roads with the windows down and the music up, sun- and wind-whipped. The writer in you is unfurling. You tickle the fresh hairs under your arms, unshaved for the first time in a decade. You reclaim your body, your mind, yourself. Your hair is cut short in a country salon, you're sick of hiding away from people with love-sickened grief; you now want the world to see your face. Your smile and your strength.

You are calm and strong, powering with the writing life, diving with grace. And free from any man. You feel a much more interesting future awaits you than anything you would've had as The Writer's Wife. By walking away W has given you a great gift – impetus.

You are clean of the distraction of men now, and at peace. Because W had changed you, and that now feels like theft. You'd worn a mask, a disguise, all your time with him. As you starved yourself and changed how you dressed, as you convinced yourself it was much more important to have love than a writing life. How deluded you were and how many women do something similar with whatever their passion is. We so often re-condition ourselves from a wild, strong, openly questioning girlhood, convince ourselves that to be obedient and voiceless is the best course. Because the world around us tells us this. Men tell us, and other women police it.

And now you are no longer in disguise, you are unbound.

~

April 23rd, the intended wedding day. 'Why can't I marry W?' You ask in your journal. 'Because he has the capacity to ruin my life. To drag me down and walk clean away from it. His life is poetry and dreams. His, not mine. And he has the capacity to diminish me and I won't allow it anymore. He's a man caught by fears and it's infectious.'

Your freedom on the road now feels like exhilaration. Twinned with solitude, and somehow clean. On the other side of womanhood you no longer care about demureness and decorum because you want to live an authentic life, as a woman. You will ferociously resist being dissolved ever again. You'd been living your life, for so long, poised to become someone you never wanted to be. And you didn't realise until this time how destructive the suppression of the female psyche had been. It feels now as if a great weight of water has been pressing down on you and you're suddenly bursting to the surface, finally, you're gulping fresh air.

And you know now that if you're ever blessed with a daughter you'll do everything possible to keep the flame of authenticity blazing in her, to never have it snuffed.

~

'To never forget: that feeling of powering along the Barkly Highway with the smell of wattle pushing in and all around us, the ant hills and cattle grids and long straight bitumen strips with our tops off and new black bras from Darwin and a notebook, just that,' you write. 'Wind-whipped. Free. Completely, exhilaratingly . . . unencumbered.'

A great chasm lies between this and your former life. You could never cross back into the old one now. Love, romantic love, is gone; forever, you suspect. You'll never be so foolish again. So young. 'For to fall in love,' Colette wrote, 'is to want and need everything necessary for survival from one all-powerful and barely differentiated Other.'

You only have a few personal belongings with you now. A swag. Swiss Army knife. A fountain pen in an old Capstan cigarette tin. And courage. It feels like all you need. You are a photophiliac, a lover of light, and you immerse yourself in it on the road trip and are repaired. By distraction. As Marguerite Duras said in *The Lover*, it's not that you have to achieve anything, it's just that you have to get away from where you are.

~

You wonder: are love and creativity mutually exclusive? Do the demands of marriage spell the death of a woman's creativity? Her flinty, complex, raging being, her soul? That will be one of your challenges now. To find a way to exist creatively and freely within a relationship – if you ever have one again – so that your soul can sing, still.

~

You feel feral; that this is how women, actually, are meant to be. Wild, unbound, audacious, angry, exhilarated, free. You were chosen by the wild places. You were the yes-girl, the pleaser, and you need to start looking at the more dangerous and honest side of yourself. To risk it. You will no longer be timid, or owned.

26

An elderly Greek woman once told you a wedding is just a funeral where you can smell your own flowers. You think of the solitude of love, for you were never lonelier than those times when W didn't ring. When he made you weak. You think of the savagery of it, the way it felt like violence upon your psyche. Yet there was also inner violence in the furious need to be alone. In the hatred of the tunnelled life you were walking into.

~

Back in Sydney you write to W. 'It's like everything in this desolation has become glittery and vivid. My alone is erotic, wolfish, hurting, hunting. Sometimes I plummet – burn, doubt, stumble – but there's something very alive about it all, raw and surfaced and living. It's as if a layer of skin has been peeled from my eyes. God toss me. W, I thought we had it. Yet I feel now as if I alone was holding a bright candle in the dark. And I've blown that candle out. Goodbye, and good luck.'

A difficult freedom awaits in your high flat amid the spoils of a successful, working-girl life. Stretching before you are endless, lonely Saturday nights and the questions all over again at family Christmases and all the New Year's Eves roaring with solitude. Your words are your comfort now, an icy blanket.

~

Yet you are gulping the world again, stepping into a noticing and it feels so long since you've been capable of this. 'The time will never come for me when there are no more discoveries to make,' Colette wrote. 'Every morning the world is as new again.' A journal is filled, then another. You're writing strong for the first time in years.

Your compassionate boss has once again freed you of the gruelling shiftwork, with a daytime news-reading job at the youth station Triple J. And you've freed yourself of men. You had to stop lying to yourself – that you'd find rescue with a man – because it's the lie the world tells every woman. You had to learn that no one could rescue you but yourself.

~

In a fever of productivity, you send off fresh short stories to literary magazines while working on your first novel. The want burns within you and won't let you go. You feel safe in this nesting writerly world, it calms and buoys you. Siri Hustvedt wrote in her autofictional novel, *Memories of the Future*, that over and over she had spoken and not been heard. You do not care about being heard during this time as long as you can write, unburdened, do not care if no one reads you. For it's the act of writing that sustains you, not the selling of the words.

~

The painter Ray Crooke said of Charmian Clift and George Johnston they literally destroyed one another, that there seemed to be this professional jealousy between them. You wonder if that would have ever been the case with W, but you never had the chance to find out.

~

But then. The fall again. Heaving, hurting sobs, late on a Friday night. You're so enormously alone. Childless with no prospects. You just want to be a mate, to someone. A sexual desert stretches ahead, a declared lifetime of flinty, barren, self-imposed exile as you wait for a future of writing and the solace of the bush, that feels like it might never quite come now.

P, your old boss who blushed in a staff meeting once, tells you that you must complete yourself creatively before you can ever think about a relationship again. He's right. You have to make a book happen somehow. You want to be your most heroic self. Couldn't be with W. The lesson you know now is to keep life simple – it feels like the secret to successful living. It was impossible with W; you existed in agitation with him.

You feel madness nibbling at the edges of your existing, cannot climb away; you pray for help, guidance, rescue. Feel the hand of God gently pushing you onward, opening you out. To the world. You firm with the writing and the painting, finding your way back into the things that still you most.

27

Four years after the relationship with W has disintegrated your first novel, *Shiver*, is published. You're thirty years old. It's been a long apprenticeship; despite you being perceived in some quarters as an overnight sensation who perhaps doesn't quite deserve this. Threaded through the novel are notebook scraps from desert sojourns, words bruised by dust that have been jotted down in your ute's cabin over many years. Notebook observations also appear in your second novel, *Cleave*.

Shiver is disparaged by an older, male critic who laments in his review that the novel can be found in cardboard display-stands by the front doors of bookshops; as if you're not being published for any kind of talent but for far more dubious, marketing qualities. Yet yours has been a twelve-year apprenticeship of short stories published in literary magazines and an aborted first novel, written in the crazed aftermath of W, which you recycle into your first two published books.

Your father accepts his lovingly inscribed copy with wry chuff. He opens it in wonder, chances upon a swear word on the first page, shuts the book and smiles. He'll progress no further. *Waste of time, that.*

~

During publication, you're completing a Master's in Creative Writing. Your class lecturer has introduced you to Michael Ondaatje's *Coming Through Slaughter,* which enters your world like a depth charge of possibility. You carry that battered paperback for decades; the pages are almost greasy from being dog-eared and scribbled upon. For years this slim book coaxes you into audacity.

The middle-aged, greying lecturer says nothing in class as your novel is published. Then the review appears, from the man who takes umbrage at your perceived, unearnt position by bookshop entrances. Now is the time finally for your lecturer to comment. He reads out to the class the cruellest aspects of the review. You can still remember his chuckly glance across at you, to see how you're taking it; this public humiliation from a middle-aged man of no note before you; you must be a good sport, eh, come on, chuckle along with us. You can still remember the mortification burning through you as he read out his carefully chosen words to the class – the worst of the piece. Can still remember your flaming cheeks. The lesson:

you don't deserve this and you might as well stop your writing career right now, eh. And all this from an older man who's teaching and not writing himself; who has, of course, never published a book. The audacity. Of you. The voice. Of you. How dare you.

An early profile as a young novelist declares upfront you have self-belief; the male writer makes it sound like an insult. Makes you feel there's something wrong in a young woman believing she could trespass into the hallowed world of books. And because of that kind of sneering, early in your career, you almost convince yourself you aren't good enough. The headwinds feel icy and strong. Your own ego is so fragile and these men cannot see it; or perhaps they do and scent blood. It feels like imposter syndrome writ large; and is it any wonder women suffer from it more than men?

~

Years later you write a column in Australia's national newspaper, at its invitation. You accept the gig to buy precious time for what you love doing most – writing novels. Some male readers, many, are affronted by your words in their hallowed space; they make you feel this is not your place and the sooner you disappear from it the better. The sneering reaches its crescendo week after week in the reader comments published under the online version of your column. The implication: these readers want you to stop. They want to halt you asking uncomfortable questions, with their little stabs of truth, because you and so many other women's voices are upsetting the apple cart of the patriarchy. The newspaper keeps you on.

From a male reader who is indicative of so many: 'All I can say after reading your latest mentally ill dribble in *The Australian* is that you are "JUST" a fucking idiot.' The intention is to bully you into giving up but it only makes you more determined. Because you're getting under their skin, hitting home. The attempt at erasure can come from an anonymous male reader of your column, or a lecturer at university. The intention feels the same.

~

Sylvia Plath wrote that the worst enemy for creativity is self-doubt. Yet as females, and as female artists, self-doubt is our anguished bedfellow – traditionally we're made to wallow by the gatekeepers to a creative professional world. Throughout history female artists have been made to think how dare you even think you can join this world. Question. Succeed. Ted Hughes, after Plath's death, wrote movingly about the woman hated, belittled and scorned by the establishment. In his *Birthday Letters* he wrote how she met 'the mystery of hatred'; how 'they' let her know, day by day, the contempt for everything she attempted. She had enormous courage to keep going, to strap herself to the god of creation because she had to. She couldn't give up no matter what was flung her way.

~

Rebecca Solnit wrote in *Men Explain Things to Me* that credibility is a basic survival tool. Throughout your career people have tried to strip you of it. Sneered that you somehow got a leg-up, weren't worthy, weren't good enough, have no right to be in their space. Yet your voice is your weapon and you will keep using it as long as you can.

Jenny Offill, in *Dept. of Speculation*, wrote of the fabled art monster who never got married and immersed themselves in their creative life instead, something women rarely become because these monsters only concern themselves with art and rarely the mundanities of domestic life. Offill points out that Nabokov didn't even fold his umbrella and his wife, Véra, licked his stamps for him. Yet how to find the happy medium? A man confident enough in himself to not dissolve you within a partnership. A man confident enough to let you be who you really want to be, to let you do what you really want to. A man comfortable enough with ironing his own shirts.

~

At the age of thirty-two you ask a good man to marry you. You're ready now. Clear-eyed. It's taken a long time to brew a world that will work for you, a singular world outside the parameters of a traditional marriage. This good man will not break you, you sense that. He is kind. And he will give you the greatest blessing you could ask for – freedom.

He respects the creative spirit and is chuffed when you succumb to it. He's the only type of man you could be with now. Avowedly beta and utterly content with it.

He says yes.

It feels like God's hand, on your shoulder.

28

Celia Paul eventually marries, years after her relationship with Lucian Freud. Her husband, Steven Kupfer, lives a few miles away from her. They maintain separate living spaces. Paul makes it clear she needs her private space and Kupfer happily accepts it; she is the female art monster who has married. She found a way, and to you it seems like the perfect, longed-for arrangement. She explained in an interview that the two of them go out to supper several times a week, and her husband rings her punctually twice a day. 'Compared to Lucian,' she said, 'having that support is extraordinarily confidence giving.' As artists, women have to find men who will give them confidence, and who are confident within themselves. To let them go.

~

Georges Bataille wrote that the need to go astray – to be destroyed – is an extremely private, distant, passionate and turbulent truth. Your greatest blessing is to have found a man who says just go, write, get out of here, whenever he senses the crammed world of domesticity closing over you. So that you are righted. For him, and for yourself, but most importantly for the children you have together. So that you're a better mother in the long run.

Right now you're writing these words in a café while your husband holds fort at home. He knows he'll get a better, looser, more relaxed wife in return if he gives you the space to do what you really want to do; it will give him the woman he fell in love with. She is disappeared if she cannot write. The damning line from Turgenev – 'I could not simplify myself' – haunts us as women, as wives, as working mothers. Because we may be raging inside to do something we're not able to, because we can't carve out the space. Once you were going to marry a writer yet you know you wouldn't be writing today, to the extent you do, if that marriage had gone ahead. As a writer you had to break from the writer, to write.

~

In *A Room of One's Own* Virginia Woolf talks of an absence of hatred, bitterness and fear that informs the works of William Shakespeare. 'The mind of an artist, in order to achieve the prodigious effort of freeing whole and entire the work that is in him, must be incandescent, like Shakespeare's mind, I conjectured . . . there must be no obstacle in it, no foreign matter unconsumed.' Yet a woman's mind is usually always impeded. By children, by men, by domesticity's taunt. To write we need curiosity for the world and money and freedom – from all those things that usually swamp us.

Woolf was lucky. She was childless with a supportive husband and a generous yearly legacy from an aunt. 'No force in the world can take from me my five hundred pounds . . . Food, housing, and clothing are mine forever. Therefore not merely do effort and labour cease, but also hatred and bitterness. I need not hate any man; he cannot hurt me. I need not flatter any man; he has nothing to give me.' Woolf was free. To be honest and audacious.

~

You can no longer wander through Paris's Picasso Museum with the fug of admiration that you did in blinkered youth. Now you see masterpiece upon masterpiece (noting the gender bias in that very word) of jagged, broken women; lovers fractured and cleaved and eviscerated; women made ugly. Where is the tenderness? 'Women are machines for suffering,' Picasso told Françoise Gilot, one of his many muse/mistresses, and it's an attitude saturated through his art. His granddaughter, Marina, spoke of how much her family had suffered under him. 'He needed the blood of those who loved him.'

And what of the muse who attempts to break free from control, to find her voice and to exercise her own audacity? The male artist tries to break them, again and again. It's in Andy Warhol's increasing belittling of Edie Sedgwick, who eventually committed suicide. It's in Ernest Hemingway as he railed against his writer wife, Martha Gellhorn, whose absences when she was on assignment during World War II infuriated him. When she covered (magnificently) the Italian Front, Hemingway wrote to her, 'Are you a war correspondent, or wife in my bed?' He then went to the front just before the Normandy landings; she did too, despite Hemingway trying to block her travel. Later in life Gellhorn insisted in interviews that her former husband's name never be mentioned. 'I've been a writer for over forty years. I was a writer before I met him and I was a writer after I left him. Why should I be merely a footnote in his life?' The male 'genius' got his petty revenge in print, post divorce, when he wrote a poem, 'To Martha Gellhorn's Vagina', comparing it to the wrinkly neck of an aging hot water bottle.

Why isn't a female allowed to be the lauded artist – the 'genius' – alongside the males colonising that hallowed space? As opposed to the blank slate of a girl who's meant to be vacant, compliant, subservient, waiting for her man in bed and kitchen; an object to be looked at, exploited, consumed? The idea of muse doesn't give space and energy to the full-blooded woman roaring ahead with her own wants, her own needs and talents. It implies something lesser.

It was a woman – Sybille Bedford – who acknowledged the immense burden of domesticity that's placed upon a creative person's partner. Almost all her long-term loves became pseudo wives, fully inhabiting the domestic sphere to give her the space to write. 'This almost ideal setting for a writer is perhaps paid for by the future of another human being,' she said, guiltily, of her most enduring partnership with editor and writer, Evelyn Gendel. As a woman, she noticed. Declared difficult truths.

29

On your road trip all those years ago, your friend Z talked about the importance of not giving all in a relationship, about retaining something of yourself, for yourself. As she spoke you thought of a line in a Judith Wright poem, 'The Company of Lovers', about those who seek many things yet throw them all away for one thing only. And in terms of the tropes of love, well, it feels like it was ever thus – the narrative of an enquiring, independent-minded woman brought low by a man she fell hard for. Often love seems like the only way to break such a woman. And don't so many of us have a destructive, regretful, embarrassing situation in our past?

This narrative of the independent woman brought low by a man has long fascinated writers, with its passion, totality, blindness, stupidity. It's Isabel Archer and Gilbert Osmond, Anna Karenina and Vronsky, Miss Julie and her valet. It feels like a unifying, universal, clever-woman event. 'It'd be great to stop the shame,' Z told you, but it's hard, because the fall is so astonishing. To you, and to everyone else.

Yet fall women do. Desire is patient and very particular and we do not know when it will strike. But it may well lead us down paths we don't want to go, that aren't necessarily good for us, and we may not recognise the inherent dangers. Desire consumes our focus and strength until the awful truth is eventually revealed, the nub of the horror: men make us weak. And without them we can be something else entirely.

If you compare Rodin's *Galatea* to Claudel's *Young Girl with a Sheaf* – which she completed several years before the great man of sculpture finished his own piece – you can sense it's almost a direct copy. Theft. Carelessness. No wonder Claudel was driven to madness. 'In the eyes of many, I was only an unnecessary side-dish to Kandinsky,' painter Gabriele Munter said of the overshadowing by her lover. 'It's all too easily forgotten that a woman can be a creative artist with a real, original talent of her own.' What would she have been, free of Kandinsky? Camille, free of Rodin? Sylvia, free of Ted?

Yet we need our men and will be felled by them again and again, by falling in love with them. We bring ourselves undone by our own intrinsic wildness, our craving for the intoxication of passion. Tracey Emin wrote in *Strangeland*, 'My whole body craves to be held. I am desperate to love and be loved . . .' And it's as if love is the worst thing for us, at times, because of how it will erode us. This feels like a transgressive knowledge we're not quite ready for as young women. We have to pass through the fire and come out the other side, to understand. All women need the right kind of love. A generous one, that lets you be who you really want to be. That doesn't bind you or change you or use you or diminish you. That is a gift to all women, and it can be surprisingly hard to find.

~

Over many months, after the night at the Indian restaurant, your relationship with W was a stop-start of begging and refuting, midnight letters and awkward café catchups, a coming together then fresh coldness. Yet a long time down the track you were feeling maddened with sex – you hadn't slept with anyone since him. You wrote an oh-so-casual note (which took two weeks to compose) suggesting that if W ever wanted a sleeping partner, just that, well, to call you. Fool.

There was a shock of familiarity in your lovemaking, the matey tenderness of two people who knew each other extremely well. But it was sad, overwhelmingly, because as you lay in bed with this stranger you were once going to marry there was a blanket of memory over you both, muffling any joy. You were both careful not to touch in farewell, not giving each other anything to hold onto. You felt plumped with tears. Because you both knew this was it; a coming together would never happen again. You regretted your pathetic note. Why send it, why so foolish? Every bird goes in search of a cage.

That last fuck taught you that graveyard sex – sex with an ex – was a territory brimming with sadness and dust and ghosts, and it just made you feel mournful and clingy and old. The one positive was the realisation, finally, that a marriage with W would never have worked; he was the rock upon which you would break, and break, and break. Your love for him felt like black market money now; there were vast riches, yes, but nowhere legitimate to deposit it. As for those who only live in longing, well, you wish it on no one. The entire trauma felt like a necessary ritual of growing up – to truly step into the world, and live. Deeply, more compassionately, and more empathetically.

~

Would you ever again trade the chance at independence for the warm, ill-fated dream of romantic love? No. Why would you? But you can only say that in retrospect. Deep, true, compassionate love lets the individual live freely. It respects a fierce individuality, is chuffed by it. It does not try to change or snuff out the vivid spirit, it doesn't harness or break. That's not love, it's a lack of confidence. A desire to control.

After W you began to step into a new future. It was the year that stopped the silliness, that grew you up. You learnt that if you want the writing dream to happen you have to clear the space in your life and just get on with it, there's no other way. You surfaced during this time, felt too much, yet you've never felt richer and more creative. Love stopped you but it was sowing the seeds.

You published nothing while you were with W except a short story written before you knew him, because the swamping energy of his writing existence consumed you both. Now, you had a cleared path.

~

You sense that if you didn't constantly question, point out and flare up at all the little injustices you perceive, as a woman, you'd be much happier – but you'd be deadened. And that's our problem as women. We grow older, we mature, we start to think. To want. More. To be ourselves and not someone else's. Want to not be dissolved. By men most of all.

How to hold on to that blazing female from youth? When we were young and strong and shone with a bolshy light and boys were terrified of us, of our electric power. Something happened as puberty hit. Biology took over and won. Yet what you develop early on, as a thinker and observer, is a revulsion at having to serve men in any way, and you sensed even back then you would be punished for it.

But went ahead anyway.

~

You look back in wonder at the willingness to annihilate yourself for so long. The willingness to wipe the writing dream for this one thing, one only, love. How flinty and focused you had to be to become a writer. A handful of words were once spoken in a restaurant and it felt as if, from that moment, a new you began. Someone who could be who they really wanted to be. You've lived life ever since with wonder at the rescue and clarity W gave you. At the narrative of rebirth he bequeathed you, without knowing it.

After him there was a drop into the void of your future. What would you be like unshackled, unbound? You couldn't imagine. Not constantly reducing yourself for fear of offence, not being the endless pleaser, not shying away from the bluntness of that powerful little word 'no'. You're learning still and have been your whole life, and now know that by the time the exhilarating highway of audacity is embarked upon a woman is often old, and the world wants to render her invisible. You learn to persist.

You've also learnt that the great tension of your life – of many women's lives – is the knowledge that you are being punished for not being submissive enough. You are still at times being punished. The key is whether you're aware of it. You dread the controlling man, for all the females in your life, because he is the insecure man and he will want to bring a woman down, box her in – and it is a great tragedy of so many women's lives.

~

During your time with W you were a lady in waiting for the novel you would one day write; it was snapping at your heels as you contorted yourself into new obediences. You were waiting to be truly honest. Because you'd been so careful and guarded and tight as a young woman; a carefully curated self-image was so important. You would have to wait until the menopause to be truly free, in that time when you embrace the power of bluntness and stubbornness and strop. The power in stating the bloody obvious, and ruthlessly distilling your world, and walking off into fresh freedoms.

~

Your coterie of women writers sung you into adulthood. Their wisdom was a tuning fork for honesty and courage and they're all beside you now, still, in a little wooden bookcase by your desk. Their voices gave you a rope to haul yourself onward, and out, into the light. You live easier now because you're not in conflict with yourself. You have observed over a lifetime the suffocating yoke of men upon women, with everything we do, and your life journey has been in learning how to free yourself from that. It has taken decades to emerge clean of it.

~

Why do you not write about now? Because you're becalmed, and writing feeds on conflict, drama, suppression. You've sailed into a great looseness, at last, you've put your pen down on a marriage that works. Miraculously. Because there's no tension in it, and that feels like a great nourishment in terms of a writing life. You married the man who wanted to live in Canberra while you stayed in Alice Springs, the best friend and colleague from all those years ago who now gives you space and silence, to create. There was no silence with W. Silence to expand, to ramble with the thinking, to wonder and cross out and daydream and jot. W filled your mind with fret, unlike the man you eventually asked to marry, who gave you your freedom because he was confident enough in himself to do so.

His generosity hurts your heart.

Because as a woman you never expected this.

Thank you

Win McNee, Lexi Gemmell, Kay Middleby, Tina Middleby, Jennine Primmer, Vicki Harmsworth, Sally Carr, Sister Anne McGrath, Sister Kay Haesler, Jan Fox, Liz Sully, Carla Dubiel, Alison Angles, Caroline Verity, Mel Carr, Liz Clunies-Ross, Bernice Miles, Cate Cameron, Fiona May, Simone Fenton, Liz Hovey, Glenda Adams, Bernadette Chhabra, Vivien Lambert, Anne Barker, Eleanor Hall, Jo Jarvis, Selina Sullivan, Donna McLachlan, Gerry Tyson, Shannon Breen, Marina Strocchi, Alison French, Christine Tondorf, Derusha, Liz Foschia, Tracey Annear, Sarah MacDonald, Libby Hakaraia, Sue Daniel, Erina Reddan, Bronnie McConville, Jane Gazzo, Natasha Stott Despoja, Helen Fricker, Raina Plowright, Karen Viggers, Helen Razor, Jane Palfreyman, Caro Llewellyn, Margie Sullivan, Lin Sholl, Danielle Buntman, Siobhan Nolan, Sophie Sarin, Sophie Kennedy Martin, Clare Arthurs, Natalie Schevarien, Antonia Paradela, Janet Williams, Cathy

Davis, Kylie Morris, Diane Tammes, Selina Mills, Anne
Thiele, Cristina Bonilla, Kath Williams, Inga Mikulenaite,
Timea Arva, Maria Stets, Georgie Newbery, Mira Stout,
Jessica Francis Kane, Sarah Anderson, Sue Peart, Catherine
Fenton, Clare Alexander, Mary Mount, Caroline Michel,
Renee Theriault, Rachel Ratsma, Nina Robert, Susan
Johnson, Justine Ettler, Clare Reihill, Claire Simon,
Courtney Hodell, Kirsty McLachlan, Heather Godwin,
Phillipa Sitters, Nicola Crichton Brown, Gisela Stiel, Azelle
Thorowgood, Jenny Dyson, Beth Wilmont, Lee Burian,
Jacqui Roche, Branka Zaman, Issy Ker, Phillipa Frisby,
Rebecca Simor, Pip Fry, Karin Koenig, Katie Thompson,
Gabi Morden, Emelene Gemmell, Kathryn Court, Shona
Martyn, Anna Valdinger, Catherine Milne, Christine
Farmer, Jane Finnemore, Trish Gonzalez, Marion Mazouric,
Anne Vaudoyer, Amanda Blair, Christine Middap, Michelle
Gunn, Caroline Overington, Mia Freedman, Cathy Murray,
Georgie Gardener, Sylvia Jeffries, Juliet Rieden, Sally Heath,
Louise Thurtell, Zoe Walton, Christina Andreef, Catherine
Du Peloux Menagé, Suzanne Leal, Louise McElvogue,
Camilla Strang, Bernadette Mansfield, Margie Sixel, Catie
Booth, Helen Paynter, Sarah Curtis, Cath Stallman, Lisa
Huffam, Rosie Jones, Sam Werner, Tam Rowan, Deb
Grunfeld, Judy Yates, Olga Georgiou, Steph Drzewucki,
Louise Adler, Rebecca Allen, Emma Rusher, Thea Sholl
and Elayn Gemmell.